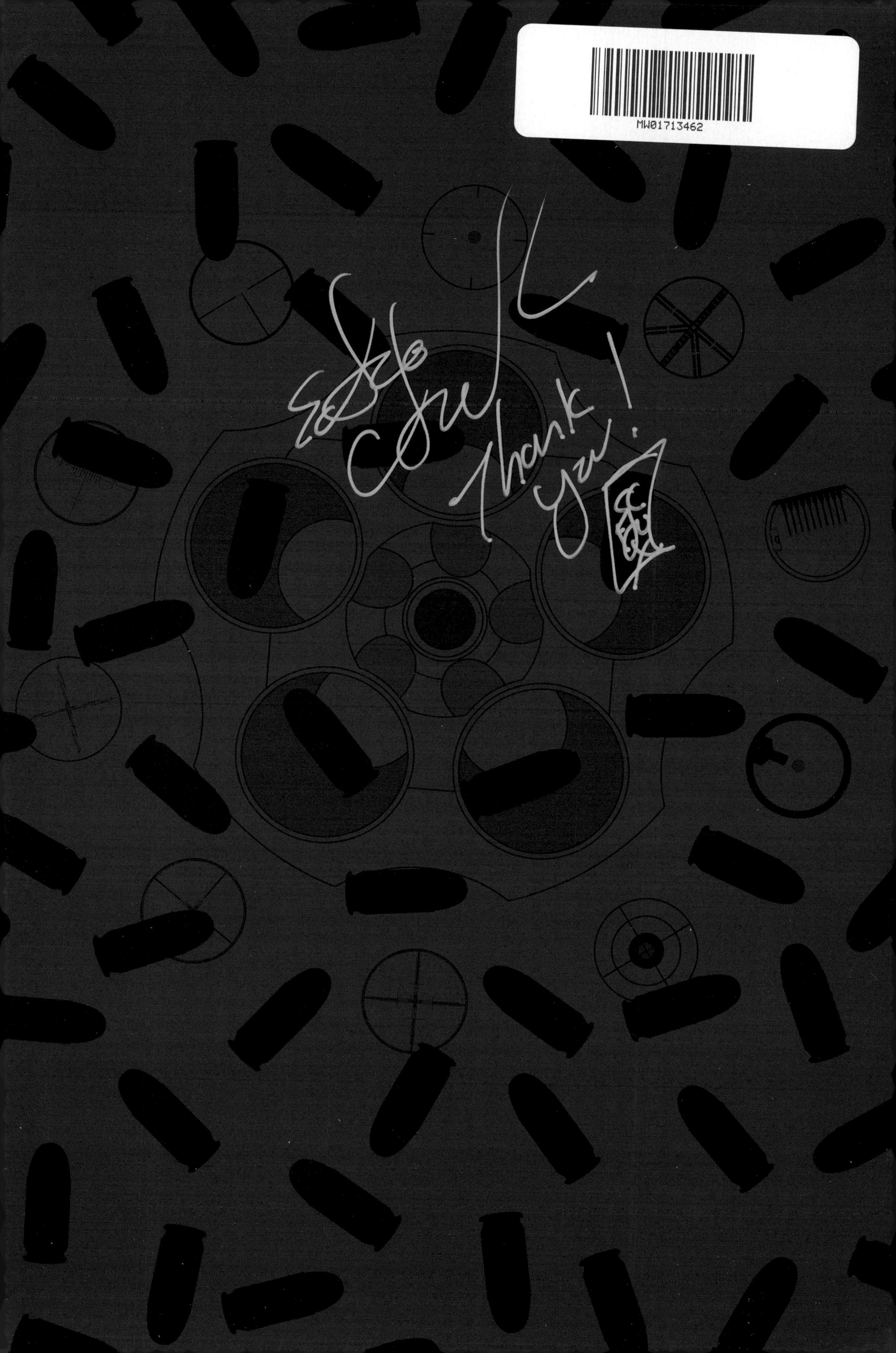

Thank you!

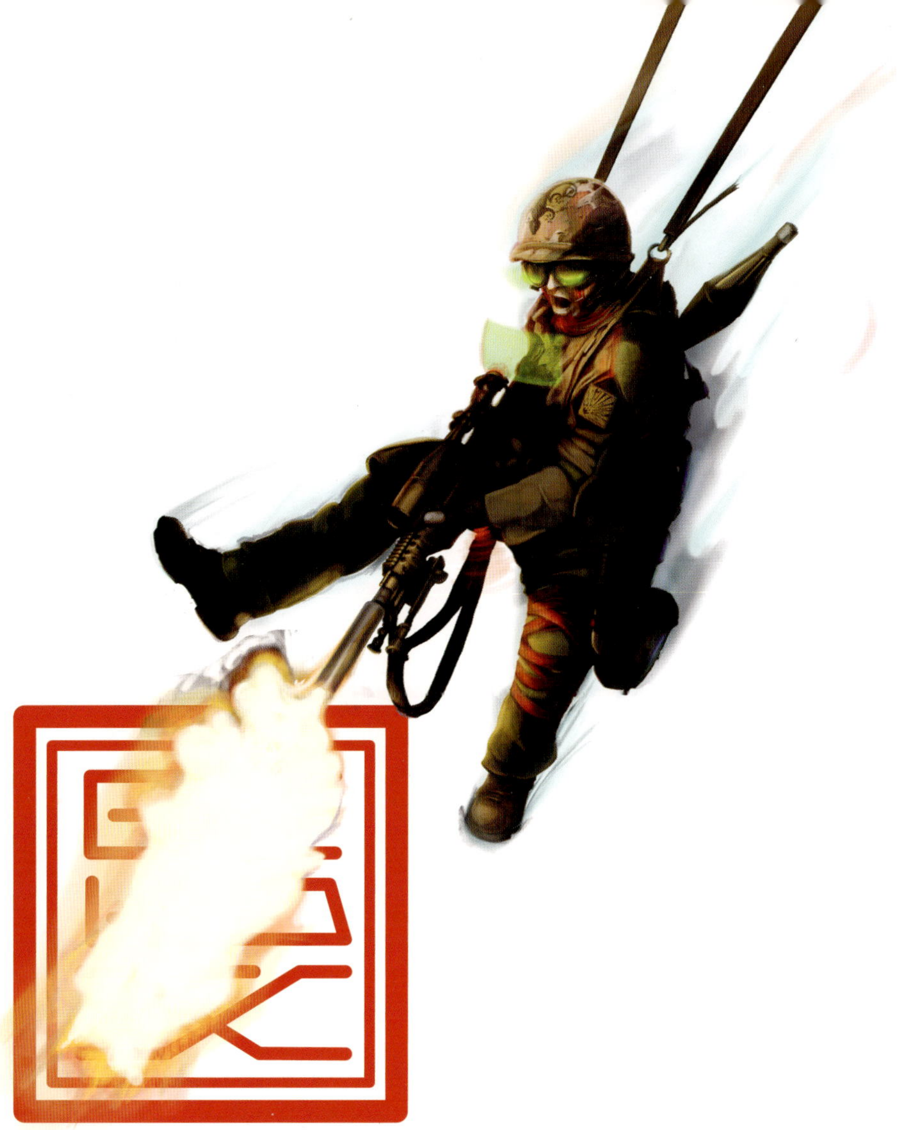

echo recoil

cyberpunk characters, covers, and concepts

To my fans, fellow gamers, players, and team-mates. Mostly to my GM.

Credits

All Art by Echo Chernik
Cover Design by Lazarus Chernik

Copyrights:	All art is copyrighted to their respective owners including Echo-X, LLC, InMediaRes, LLC, White Wolf, and Harebrained Schemes. Shadowrun™ is a registered of The Topps Company, Inc. Printed with permission.
Photography:	Echo and Lazarus Chernik
Text:	Echo and Lazarus Chernik
Editing:	Echo Chernik, Lazarus Chernik
Design & Layout:	Lazarus Chernik
Scans & Retouching:	Lazarus Chernik with Ashley Oliva
Website:	http://www.echo-nouveau.com http://www.echo-gallery.com http://www.echo-x.com

Printed in China by ChinaOnePrinting.com

ISBN 978-0-9852860-3-3

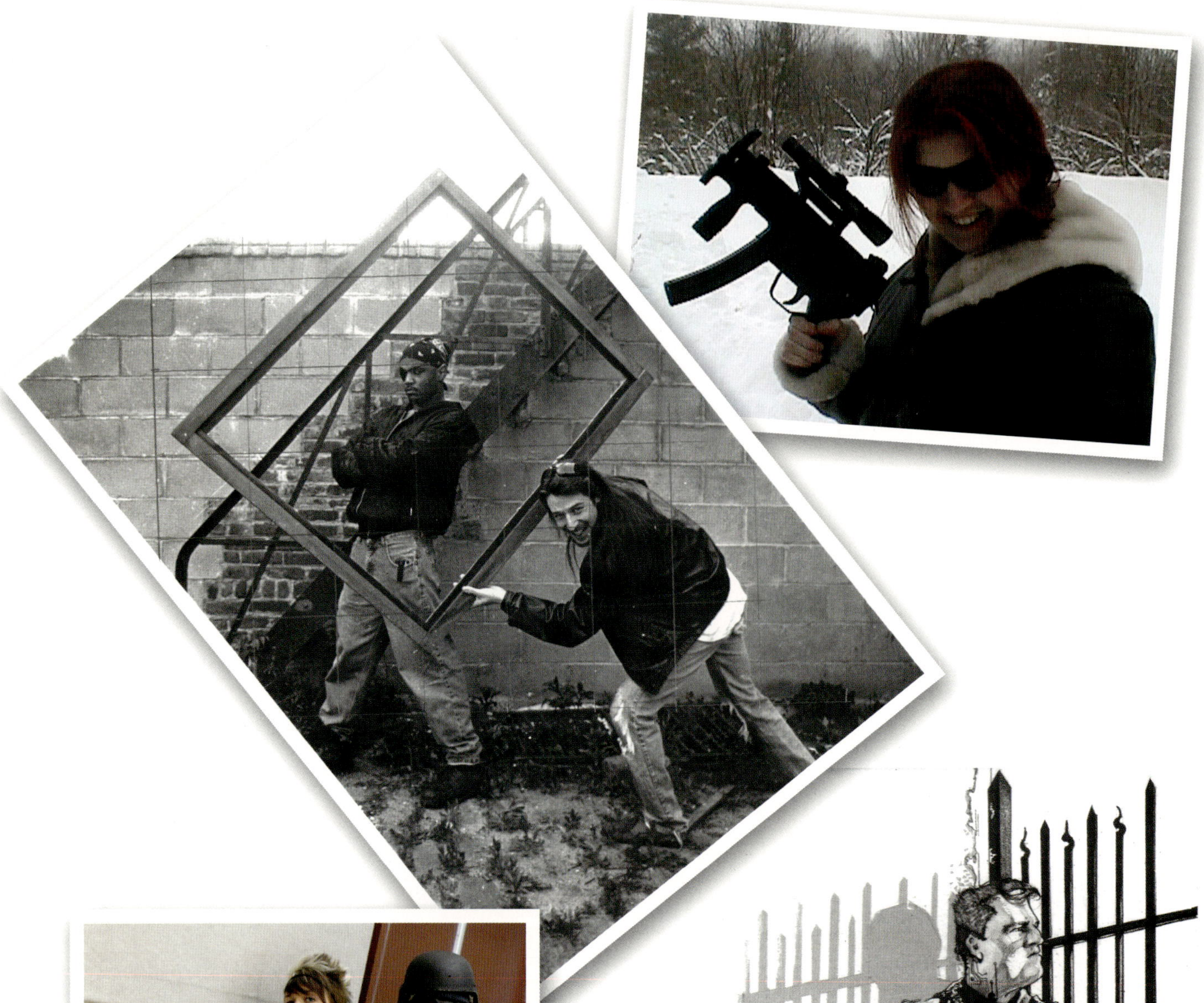

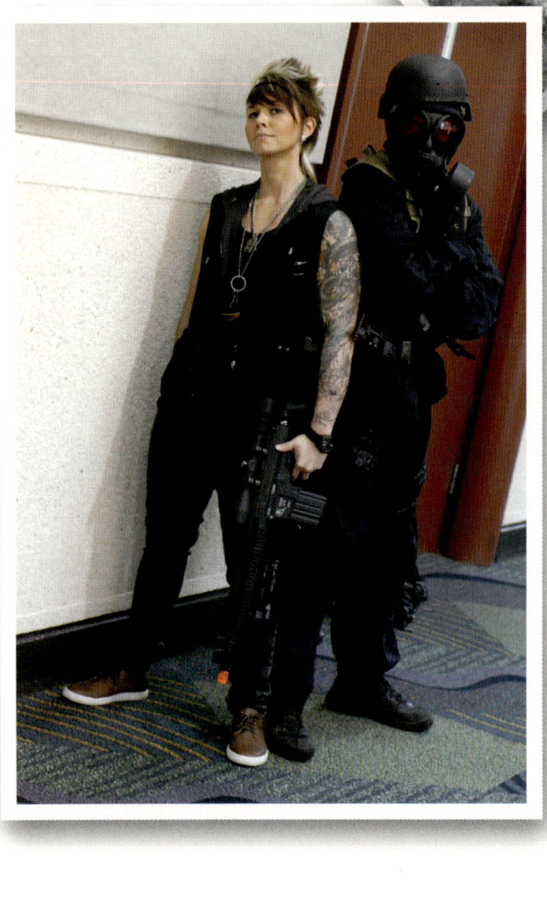

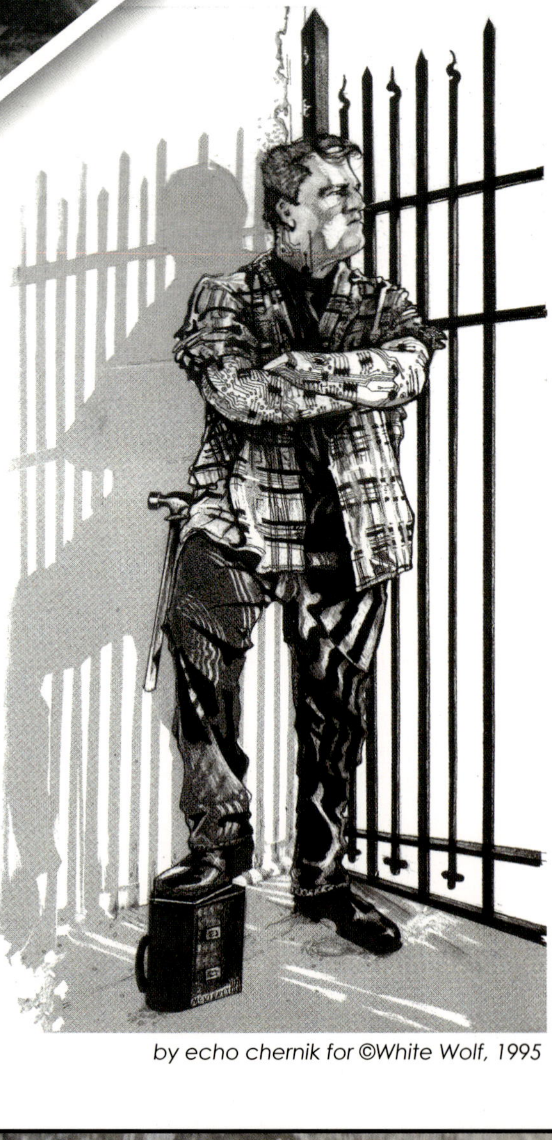

by echo chernik for ©White Wolf, 1995

Foreword

by Jeff Laubenstein

"Hoi Chummer!", as they used to say while rolling fists full of dice and dashing through dangerous streets with your gang of runners. Shadowrun is the game and its brightest visionary is a redheaded wonder named "Echo".

Designer and digital wizard, player and provocateur, Echo Chernik has blazed across the Sixth World with her singular style. Her images are sexy and fierce. Her line is sinuous and her imagery a seductive treat.

Bold and brash: Echo's art is filled with bullets and broads, rascals and renegades, elves, trolls, dwarves and orcs. Her subjects are the dark denizens of the Shadows and the lively and seductive characters that live there.

She's rocked our worlds with her sense of design, her exquisite eye and her bawdy sense of humor and I hope and trust she'll continue to chase her muse down those familiar alleys, bringing us all along for the crazy ride. So grab a fresh clip, a cool brew and some serious shades…This is going to be fun.

Jeff Laubenstein, Echo Chernik, and Jim Kitchen

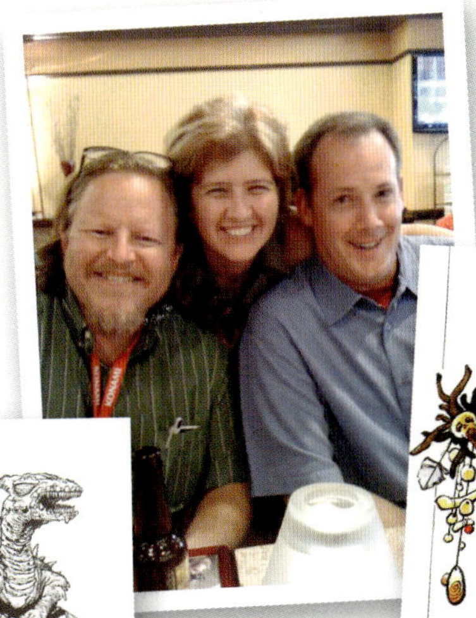

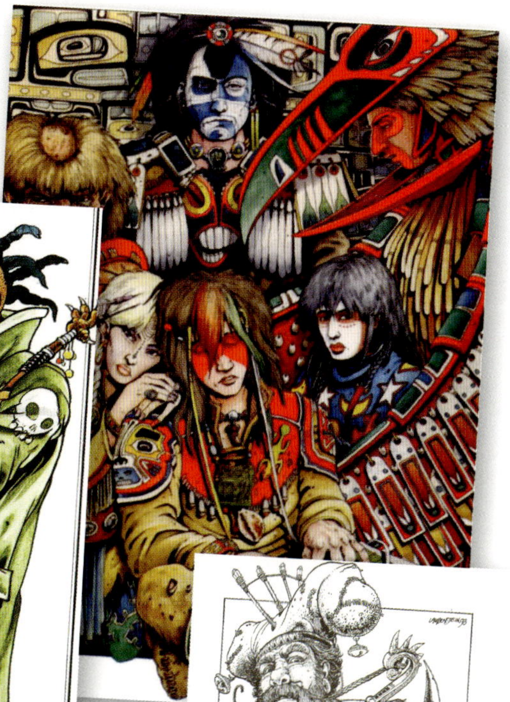

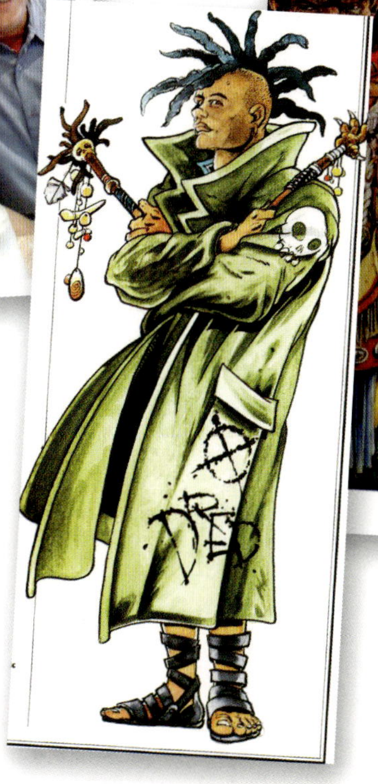

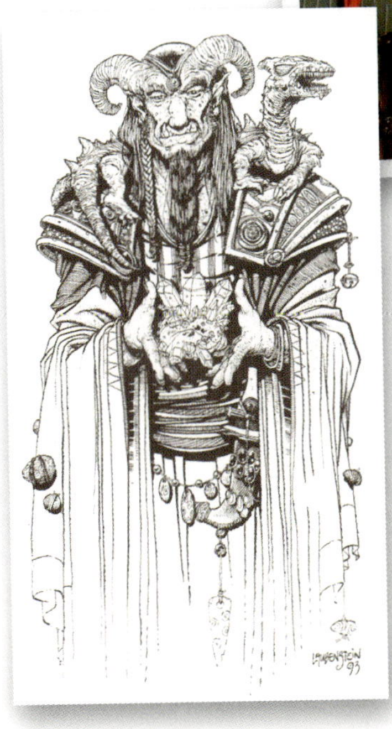

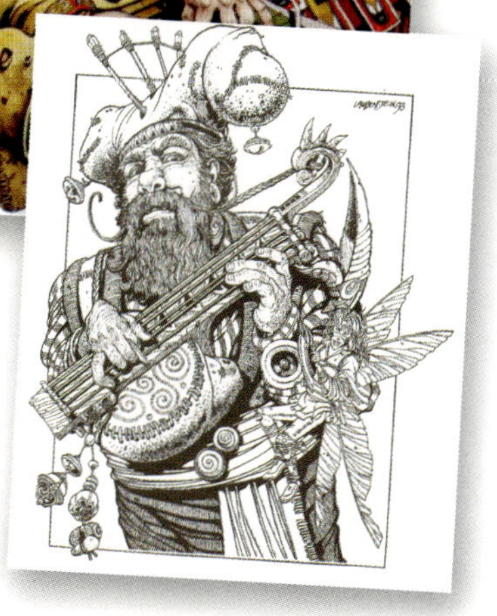

all art by Jeff Laubenstein

Before directing and creating iconic video games, Jeff was an illustrator and art director for FASA, the originator of Shadowrun. His work is the very definition of the early years of the game, and is inexorably woven into the fabric that is the Shadowrun universe. His characters are so individual, unique and rich with affectations, that I spent hours studying and admiring them. I must admit that he is by far one of my greatest influences for the game, and I strive to honor and expound upon his tone and direction in my own work. I am truly humbled by his kind words.

- echo chernik

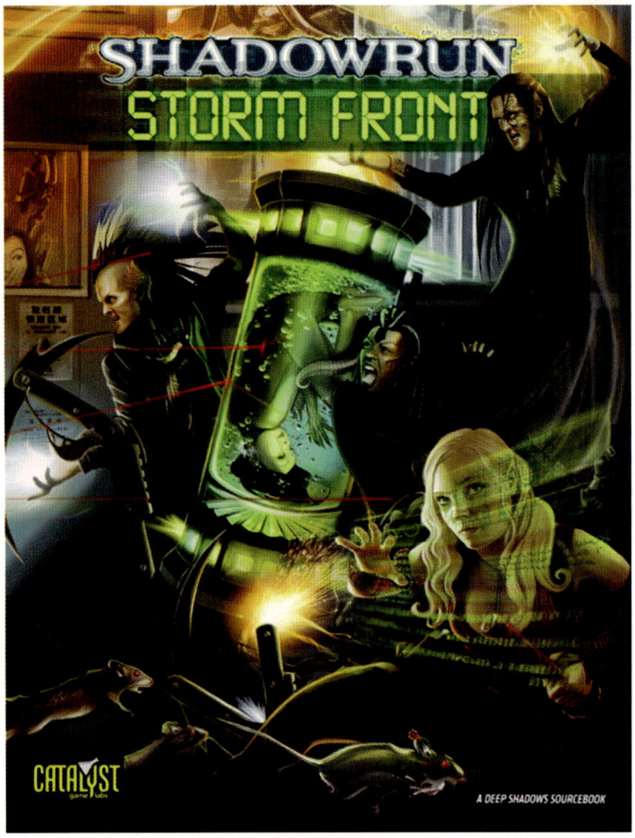

Storm Front

There are few things more satisfying than when an art director says "Do whatever you want. I trust you." That was the case with *Storm Front*. I was not given any content, subject matter, direction, or even a title. I did know that I wanted to illustrate a proper 'in media res' Shadowrun.

The term "in media res" is a Latin phrase meaning "in the middle of things", whereas the viewer enters the story at a frozen point of time during the peak of conflict. This type of storytelling allows the viewer to dissect and piece together the events that are happening, and to infer their own assumptions upon the outcome and events that lead up to the present.

For instance, you can devise that the characters are in the middle of stealing this genetic experiment, but why? Then you may notice that one of the drone's legs was shot off and it is being partially held up by a runner shouting for help. It was probably shot off by security still aiming at them with red laser sights, but now how are they going to move this heavy tank of liquid? The hacker is desperately trying to find an exit, monitoring security traffic, and communicating with their transportation. She is calmly focused on her AR screen which is in several different languages. Then comes the question - which one of the runners accidentally opened the cage letting all of the experimental plague mice loose? (Can you find all seven?)

As an actual player of the game, I like to add history and depth to my pieces that entice the viewer to imagine and create the backgrounds and motivations of the characters. Certain details specific to the universe help to enhance it. For instance, in Shadowrun twins born to elves always include one elf and one human, as in the pair of brothers represented here. Why are they here? Why are they magical? Why are they expressing different totemic influences?

I shot my reference photos for the hacker and the twins in a hotel during Dragon•Con 2012. The model for the shouting team leader was shot in Orlando in 2010. The alligator girl is my daughter (then aged 7) who has gotten used to me saying things like "curl into a ball like you sleep but imagine you have a tail and look up at me like you're asking for a cookie."

My favorite part of the piece (besides the rats), is the concerned laboratory technician.

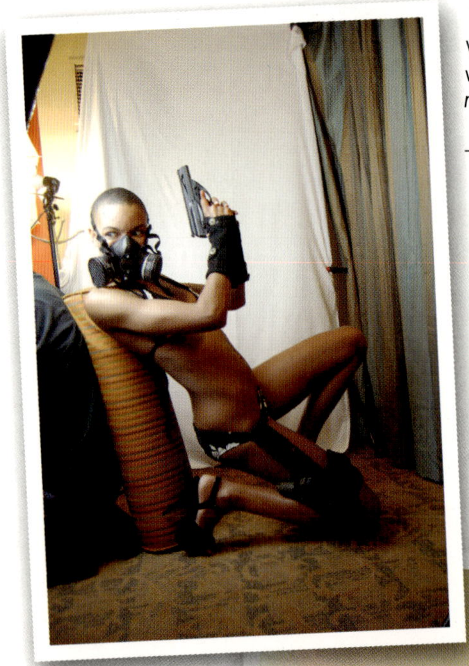

Visceral Crystal waiting for room service.

-Orlando 2010

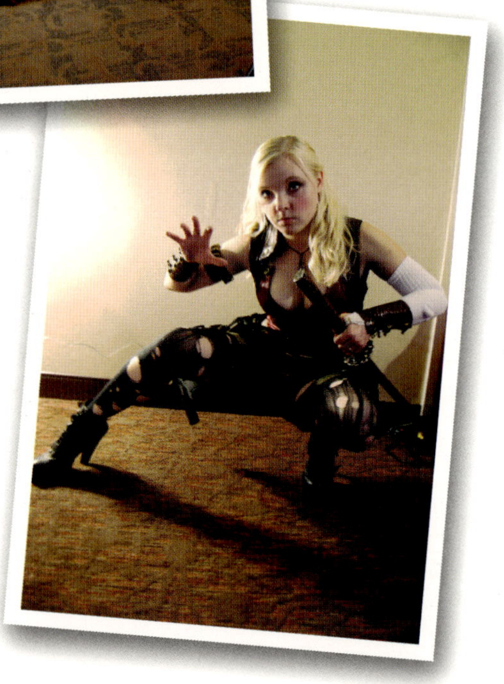

Cheese, once again focusing on things no one else can see.

-Atlanta 2012

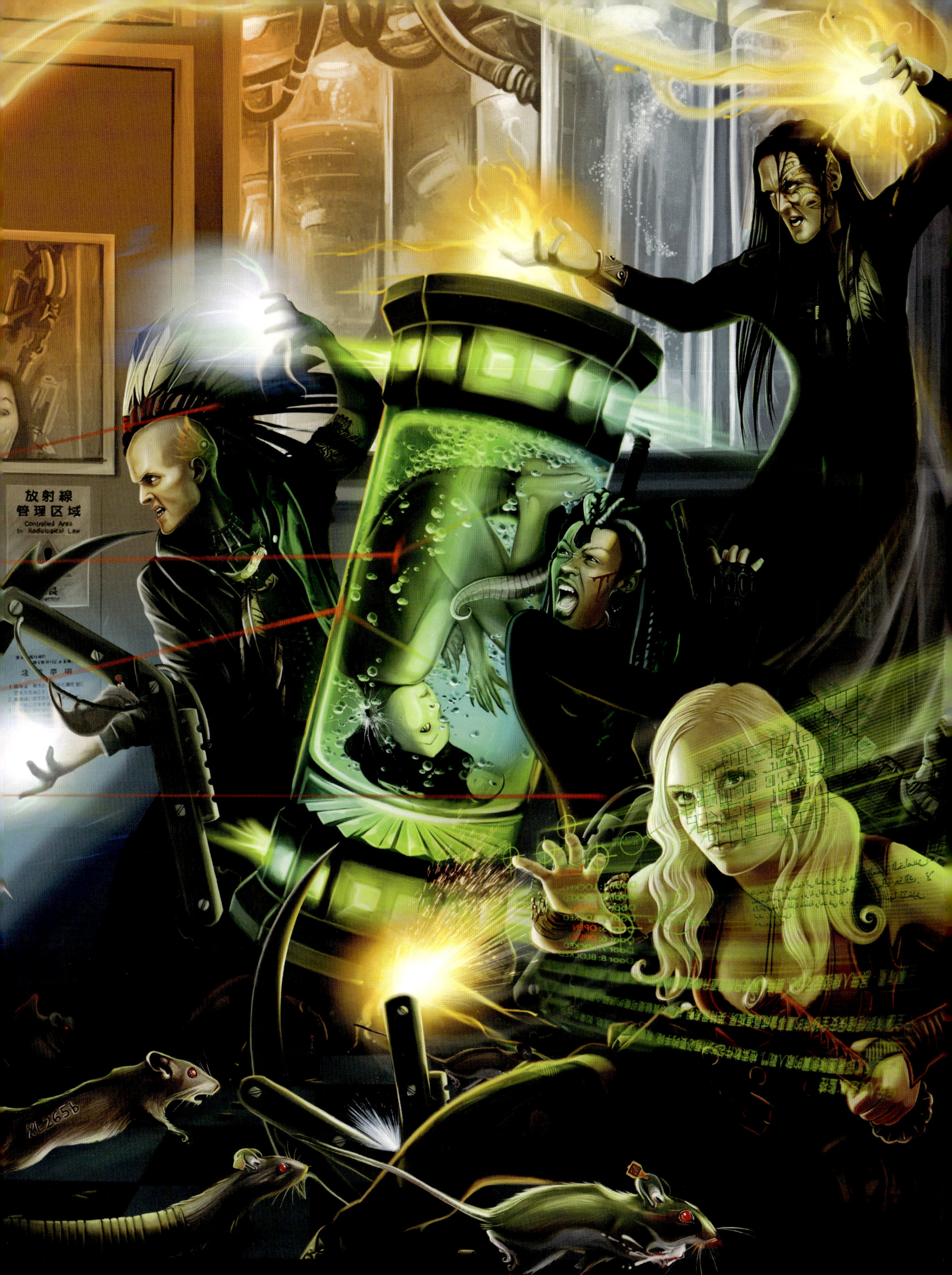

The door signs are actual Chinese hazmat warning placards.

COVERS

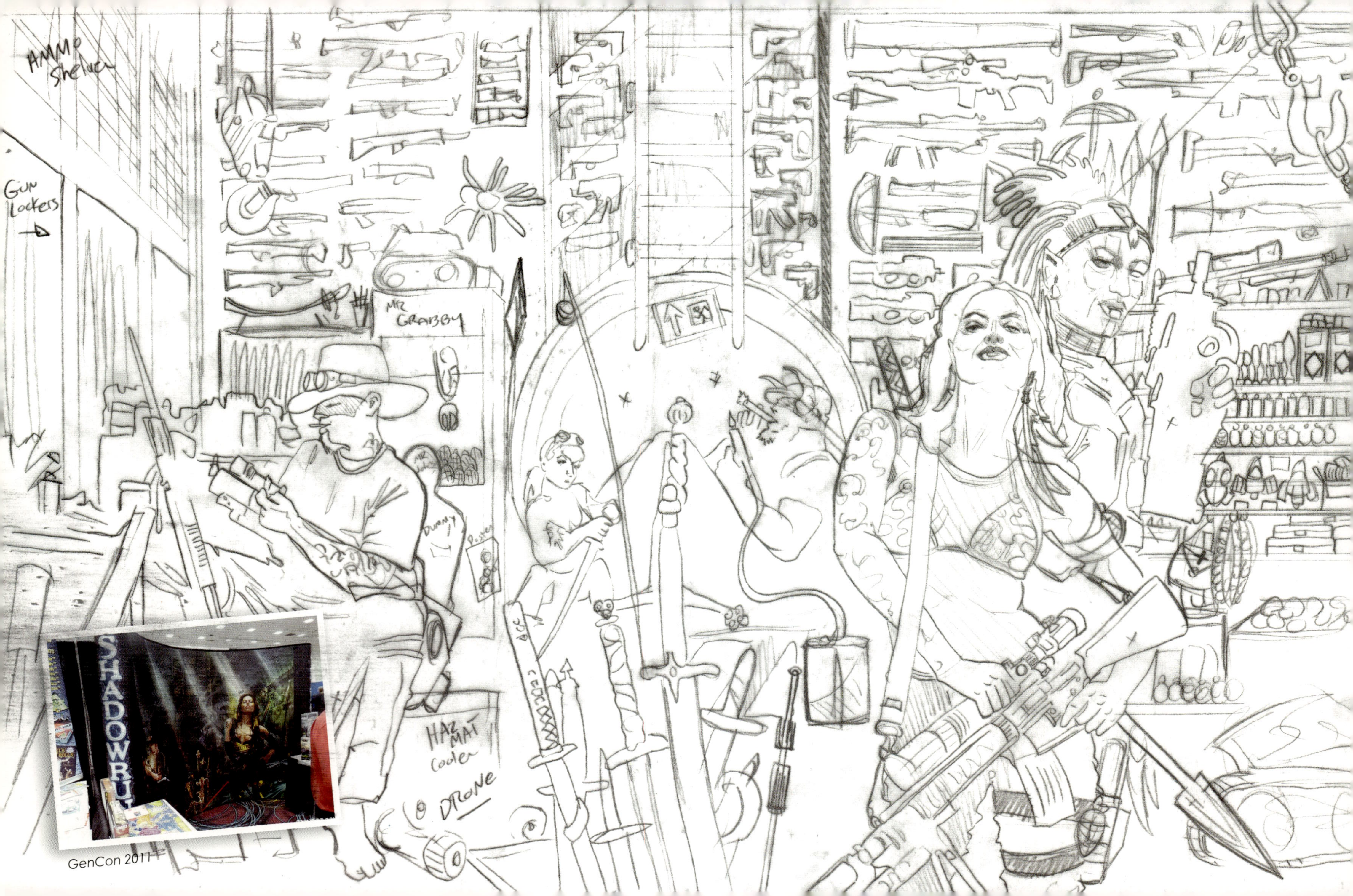
AMMO Shelves
Gun Lockers
MR GRABBY
Dummy
Poster
HAZ MAT Cooler
DRONE

GenCon 2011

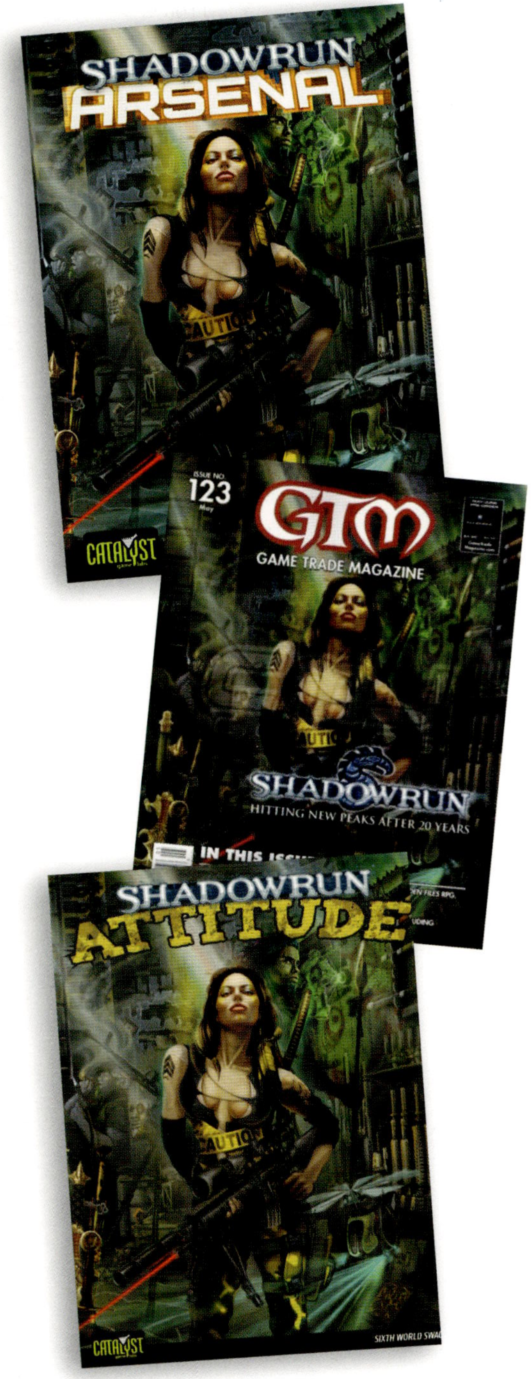

Arsenal

In 2010, I was commissioned to create the cover for a reprint of *Arsenal*. The direction was simple and pure: "Create the coolest arsenal ever!"

So, I developed a story. These five Shadowrunners are hanging out in their own personal arsenal. The viewer is an outsider and is being confronted by the leader (named Cuidado). The team is not dressed for a run. She has not yet donned her armor and the weapons specialist is barefoot. The meat is smoking a cigar and the street samurai is polishing her sword and vaguely wondering why there is a tentacle on that shelf. The warrior was shopping for armor on a hologram interface, but the viewer has gotten his attention as well. It is another "in media res" scene, as the viewer is intruding upon a nest of runners within their own home – at their own risk.

My goal was to create a cover that players could study intensely for hours. I inserted hundreds of special details that only come from active use. It's not a clean room - it's a crowded, dingy, and dirty, lair for people doing illegal and dangerous work. The ultimate *Arsenal*.

A few weeks after submission, I got an e-mail saying that it has been moved to an entirely new book titled *Attitude*. It was featured on the cover of Game Trader Magazine and eventually won the Silver Ennie for Best Cover for Role playing Supplement in 2011.

There is a story within *Attitude* questioning the main characters lack of armor which changes my illustration completely. My concept has always been pre-run and about invading the sanctity of the armory. If actually commissioned for a book called *Attitude*, I think I would have created a much more combat oriented scene illustrating a variety of different attitudes.

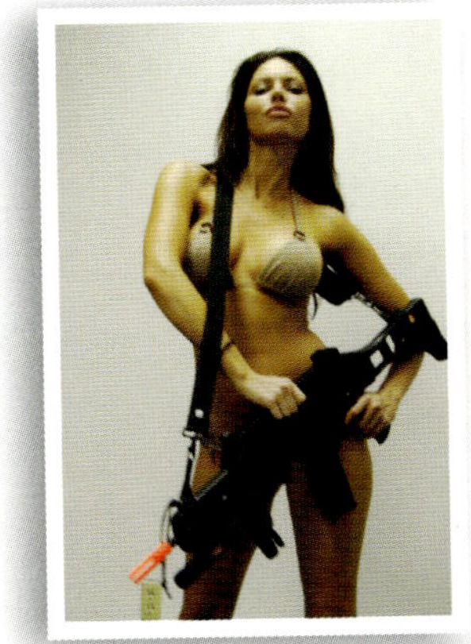

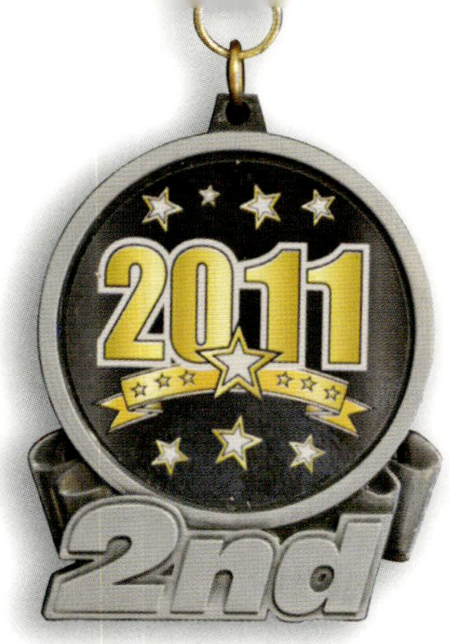

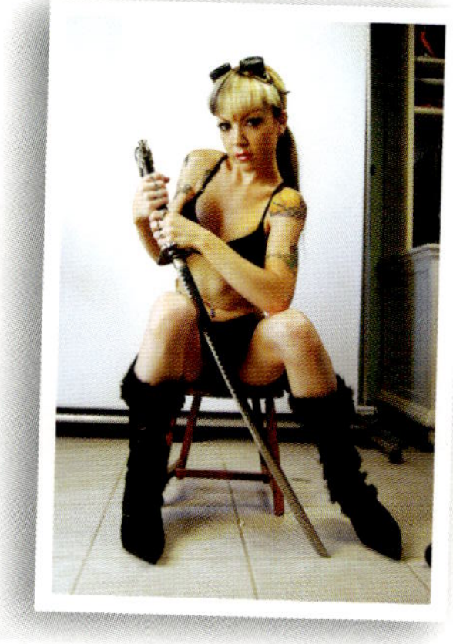

Meghan and Tara.

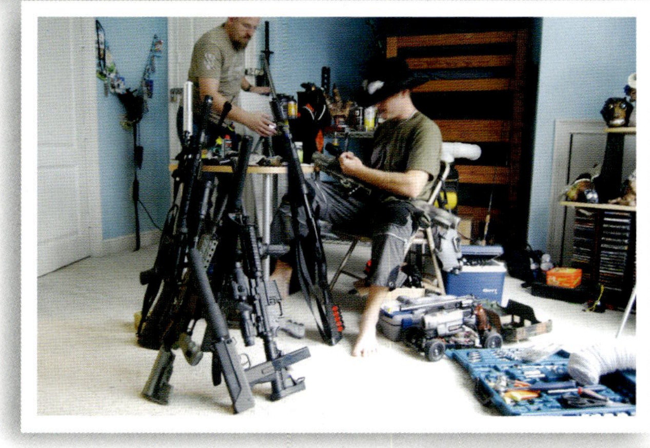

Bill (model) and Lazarus arranging props. This is actually Bill's room with his collection of guns (both real and airsoft), and tools.

That cigar was over 10 years old.

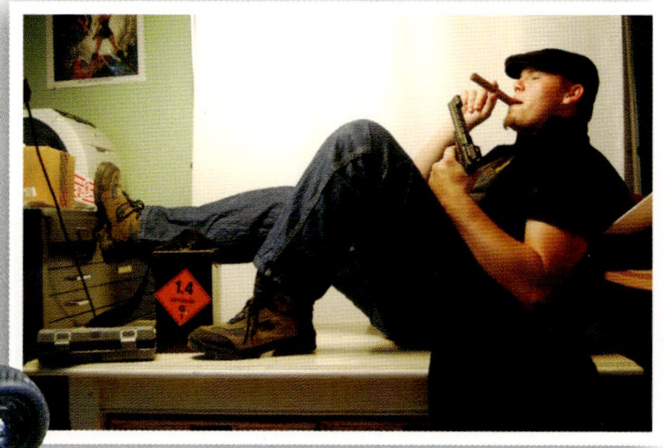

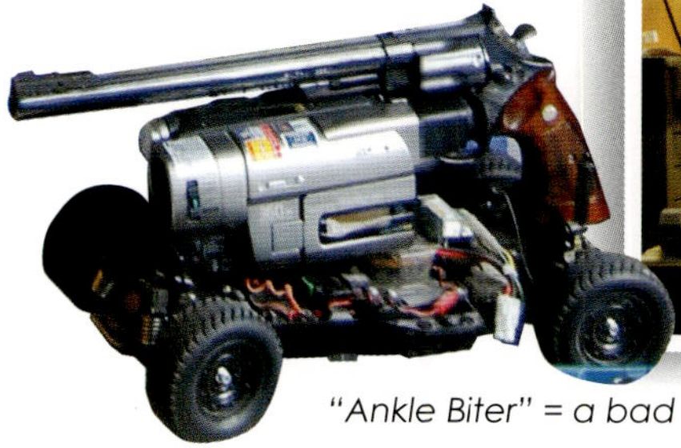

"Ankle Biter" = a bad idea out of desperation.

**It was an art department special request for Cuidado's AR-15 to have both a scope and active laser sight. I was told that Veterans from Afghanistan and Iraq used this configuration commonly. The transition from indoor sweeps to sudden downrange targeting was a must for their survival.*

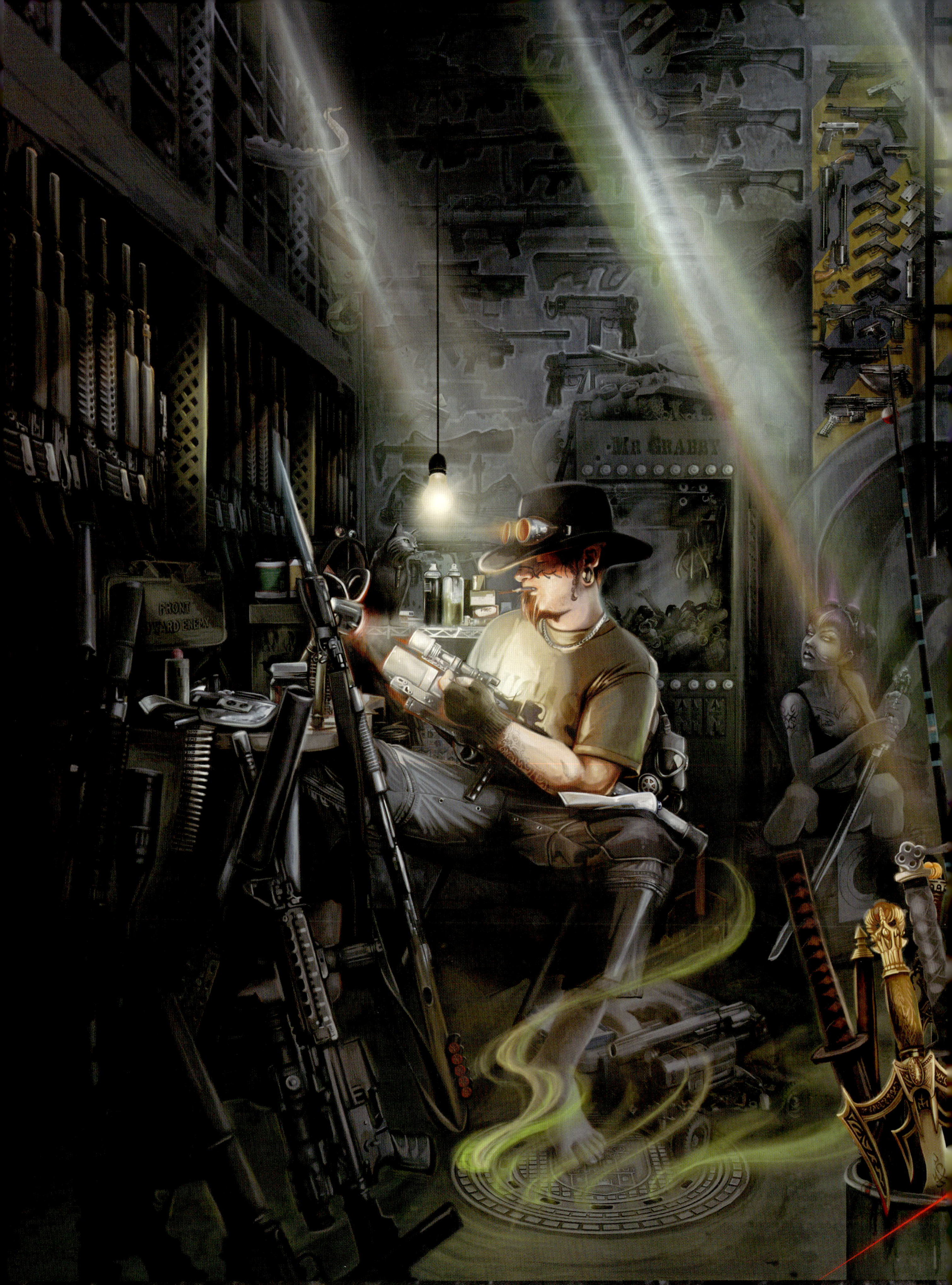

7.62mm on Collar
Tentacle
IOU and 9mm in place of G12
Ethereal Vapor
Chalk Outline
Happy Face

Fishing Pole
Ankle Biter
Flame Thrower
Mech Suit for Sale
Mr. Grabby Grenade Dispenser
Spider (not drone)

Echo-X Logo (not white)
2 Zeliskas (600 Nitro Express)
Pinup Poster of Team Leader
Escape Ladder
Sergeant Tattoo
Bare Feet

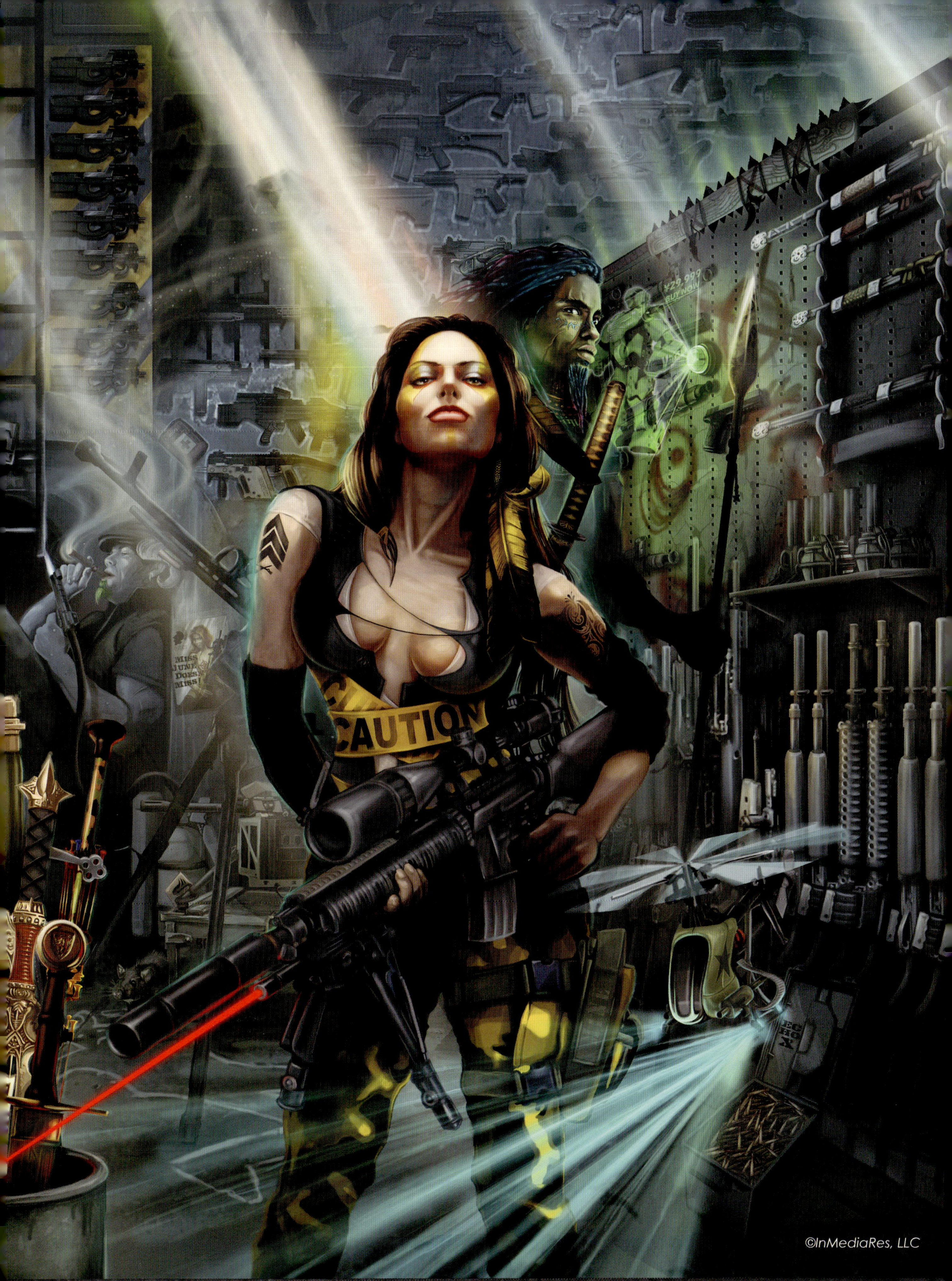

Cheap Katana
Real Katanas
Macuahuitl
Tunnel
Roto-Drone
Where's Waldo Grenade

UCAS Issue shirt
Singing Bass
First Aid Kit
Rat
Claymore
Flamethrower

Bird
Blowgun
Replica Swords
Guest Guns
Manhole cover from Prague
AAA with Tripod

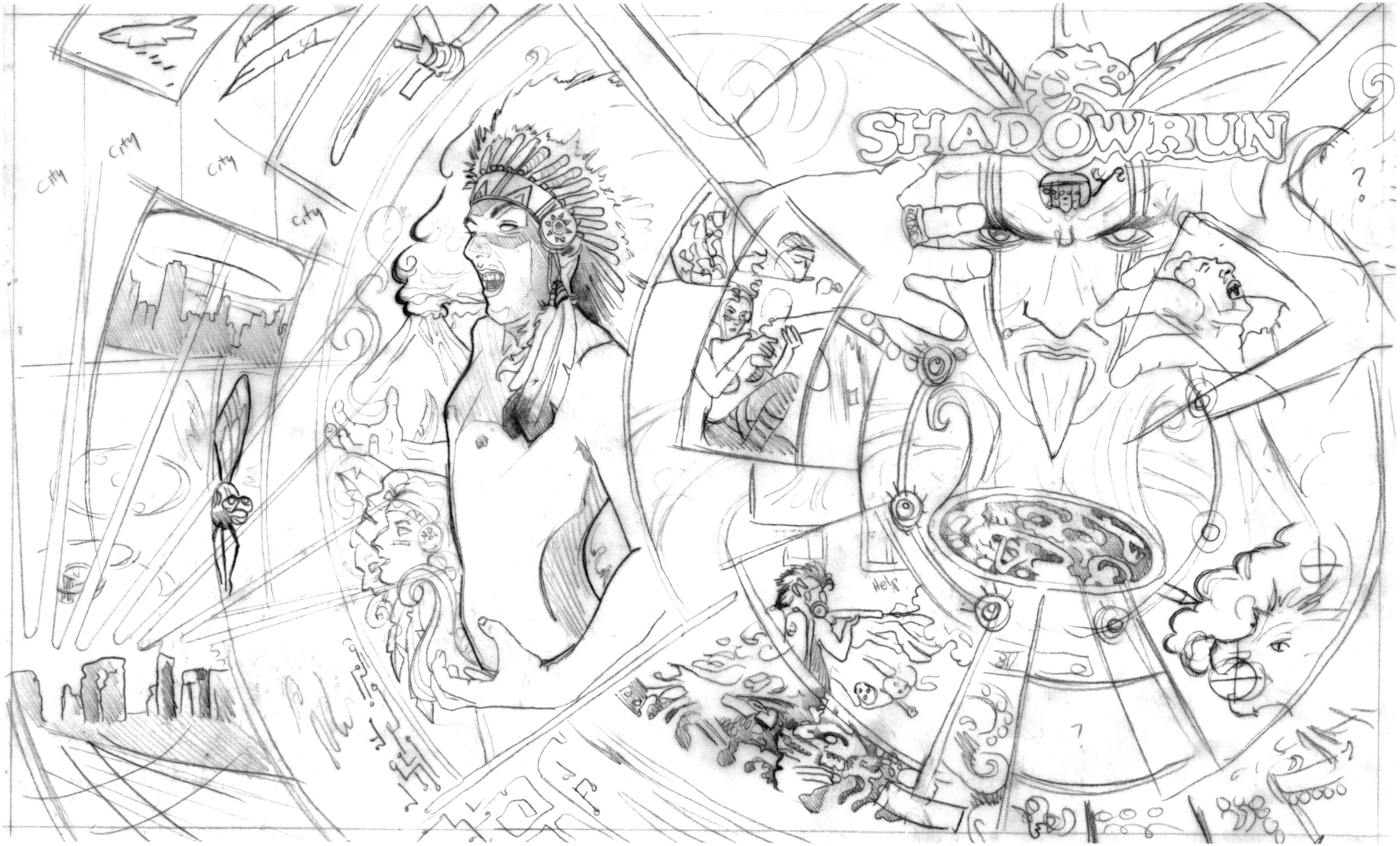
SHADOWRUN
city
city
city
city
Help

Sixth World Almanac

The Almanac is a comprehensive history of this Shadowrun universe up until the year 2072.

The direction was to incorporate the history of Shadowrun into the Mayan and/or Aztec calendar. I took that art direction to a new level and created an AR (augmented reality) screen spiraling outwards atop a stone version of the Aztec calendar.

The visage of the god Tonatiuh is the central point of the calendar. The viewer can interpret him as a spirit or an AR persona. His tongue is historically sharp to remind viewers of his need for blood, and drips upon the ancient stone, which is starting to awaken.

Having played Shadowrun for 20 years, I knew the universe, history, legendary figures, and landmarks quite well. The art notes requested specific events be included: Daniel Howling Coyote summoning at the Ghost Dance, Dunkelzahn's assassination, Haley's Comet, the Alamos 20,000 attack on the Sears Tower, Stonehenge awakening, the Corp War, the burning of the Vitas corpses, the rise of the Matrix (and deckers and hackers), Mars, Shadowrunners, and Japan, Inc.

Previous to the assignment of this piece, I had done a great amount of research on the Aztec culture for character creation in the game. I took that knowledge and applied it to really add depth to the piece. For the sun-stone I actually purchased a small replica from Epcot for reference. I then continued it outwards from the end, and actually incorporated my signature into the stone. I like how some of the gods in the glyphs are starting to awaken.

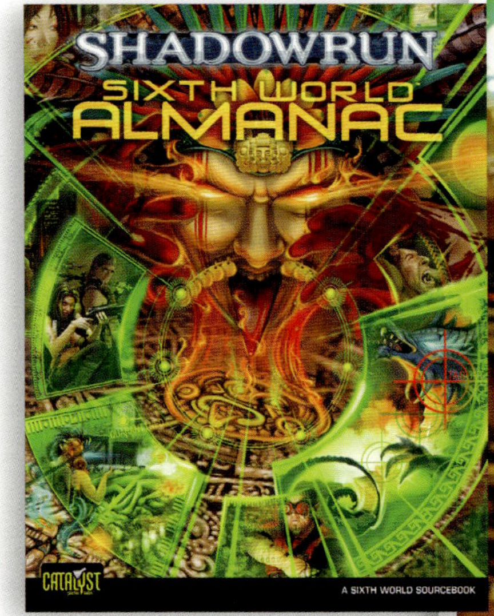

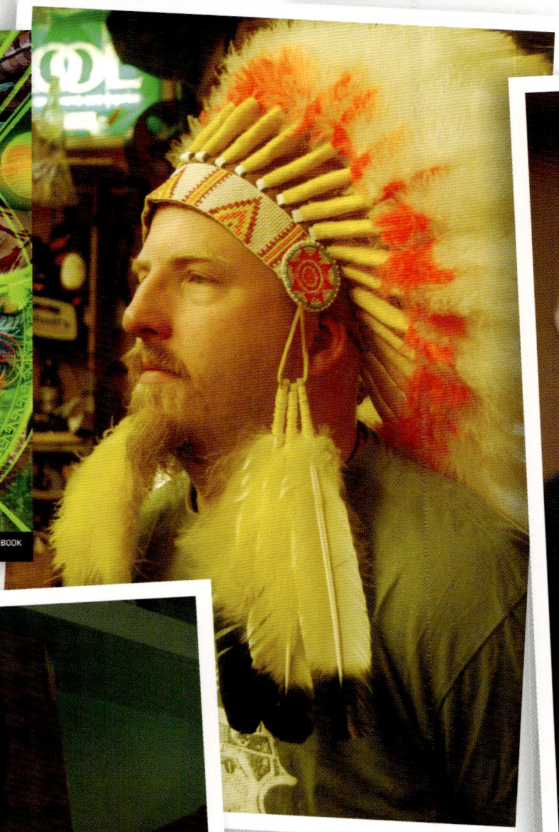

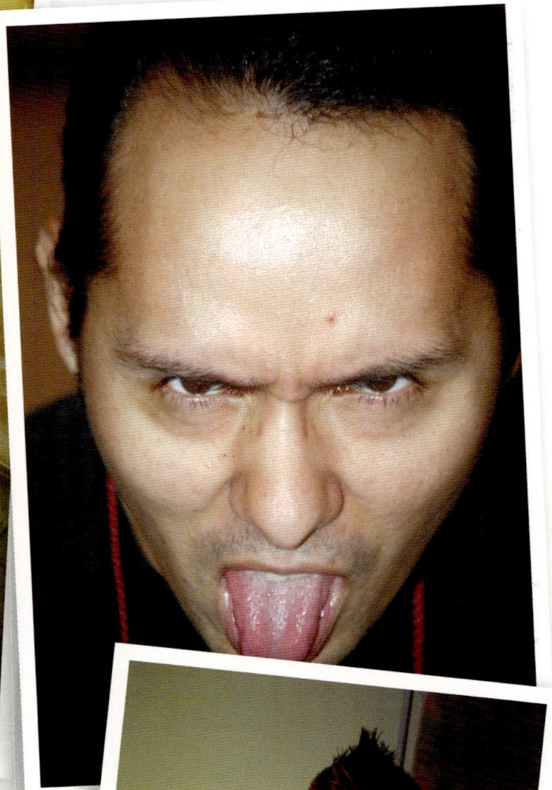

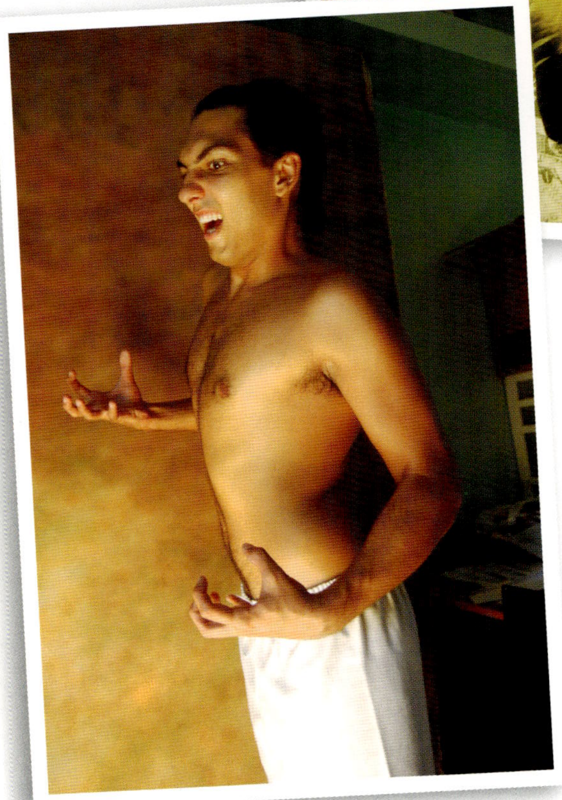

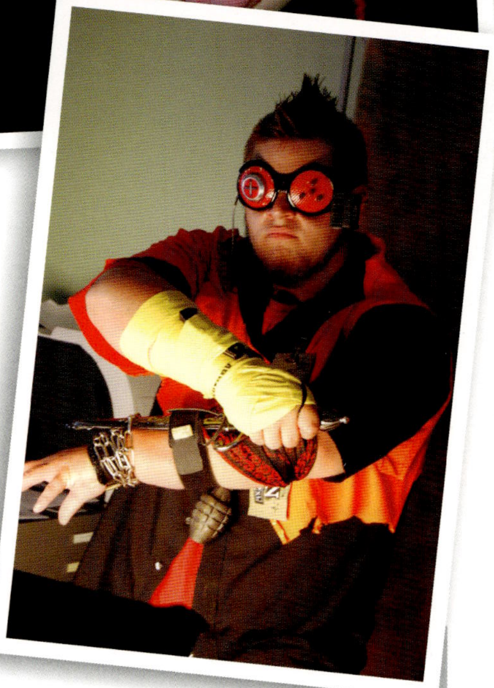

Clockwise from Left
A. Sean providing the angst.

B. Front cover.

C. Lazarus with headdress we found in an antique store somewhere in the Midwest.

D. Alain goofing around after suggesting I use a real Mexican for the Aztec God. (So I did. Thanks Alain.)

E. Bubbles as himself.

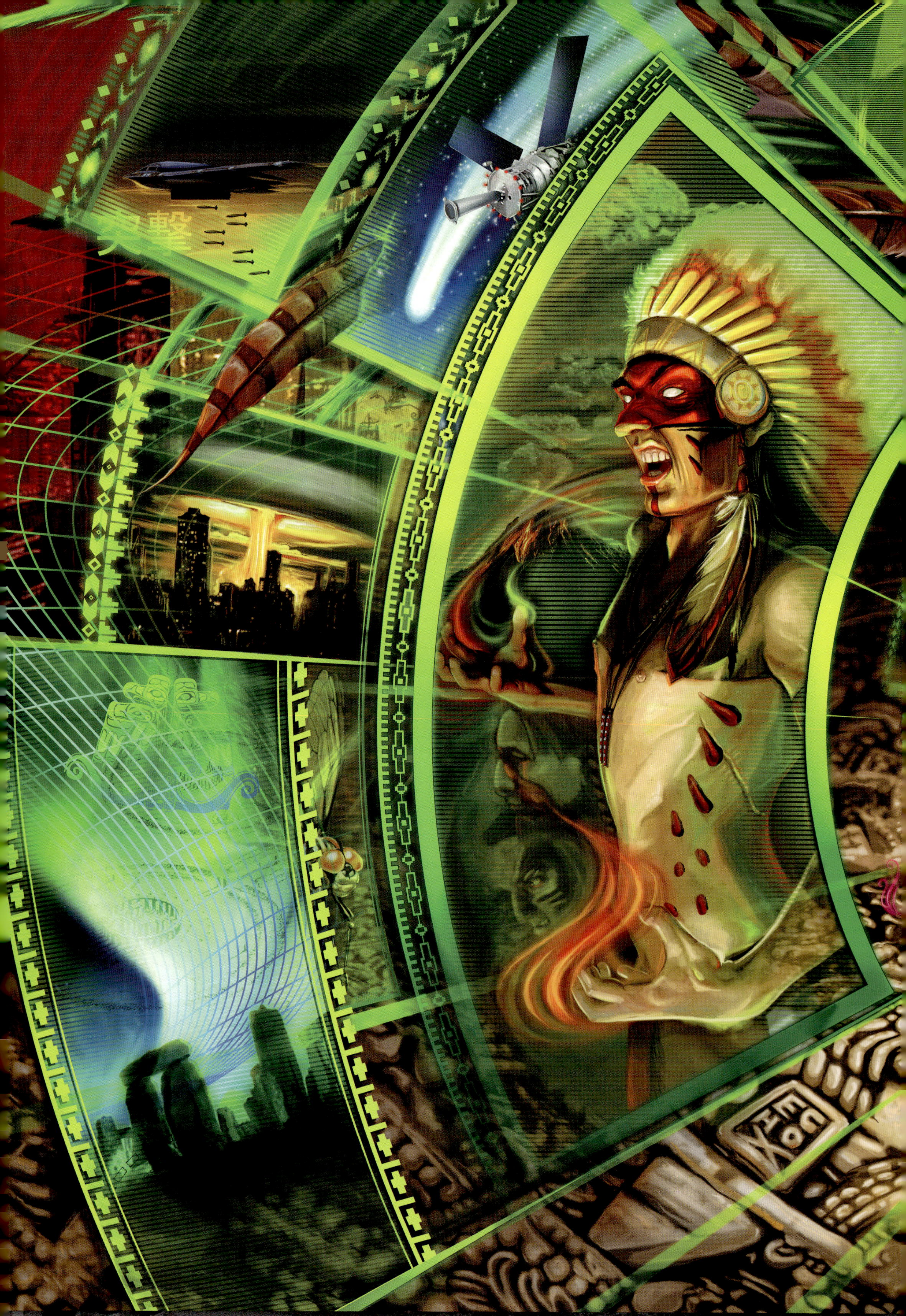
突撃

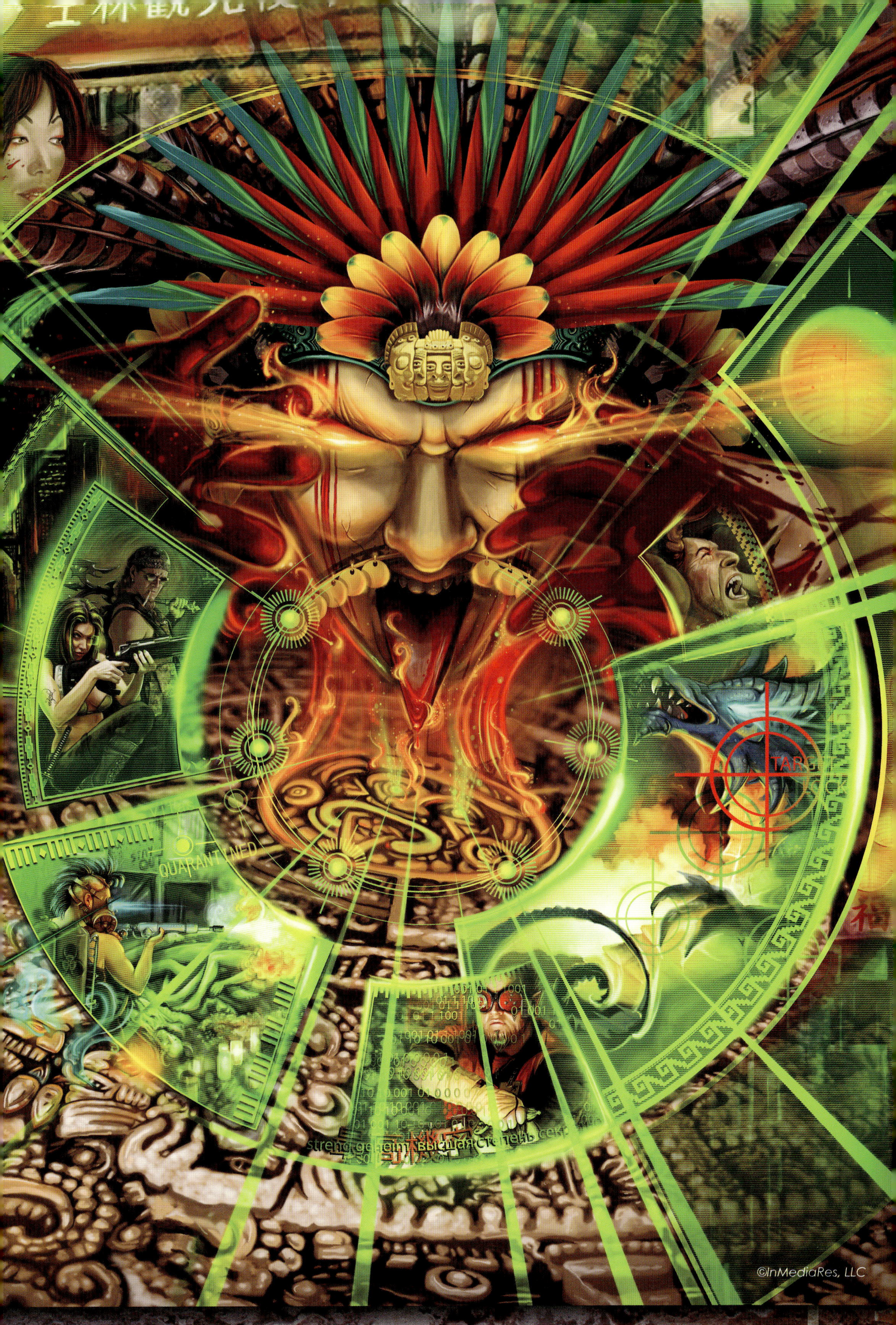
QUARANTINED

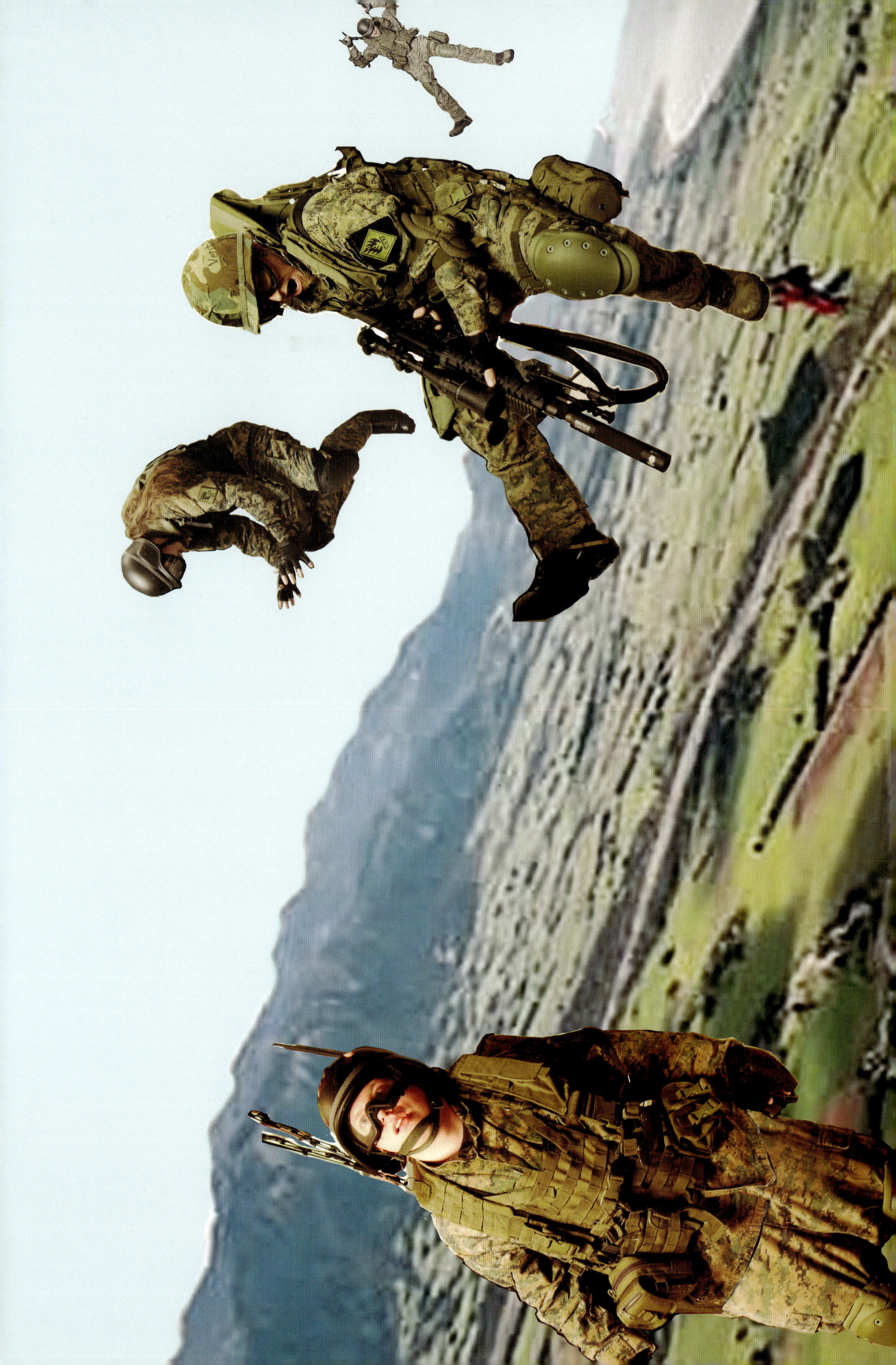

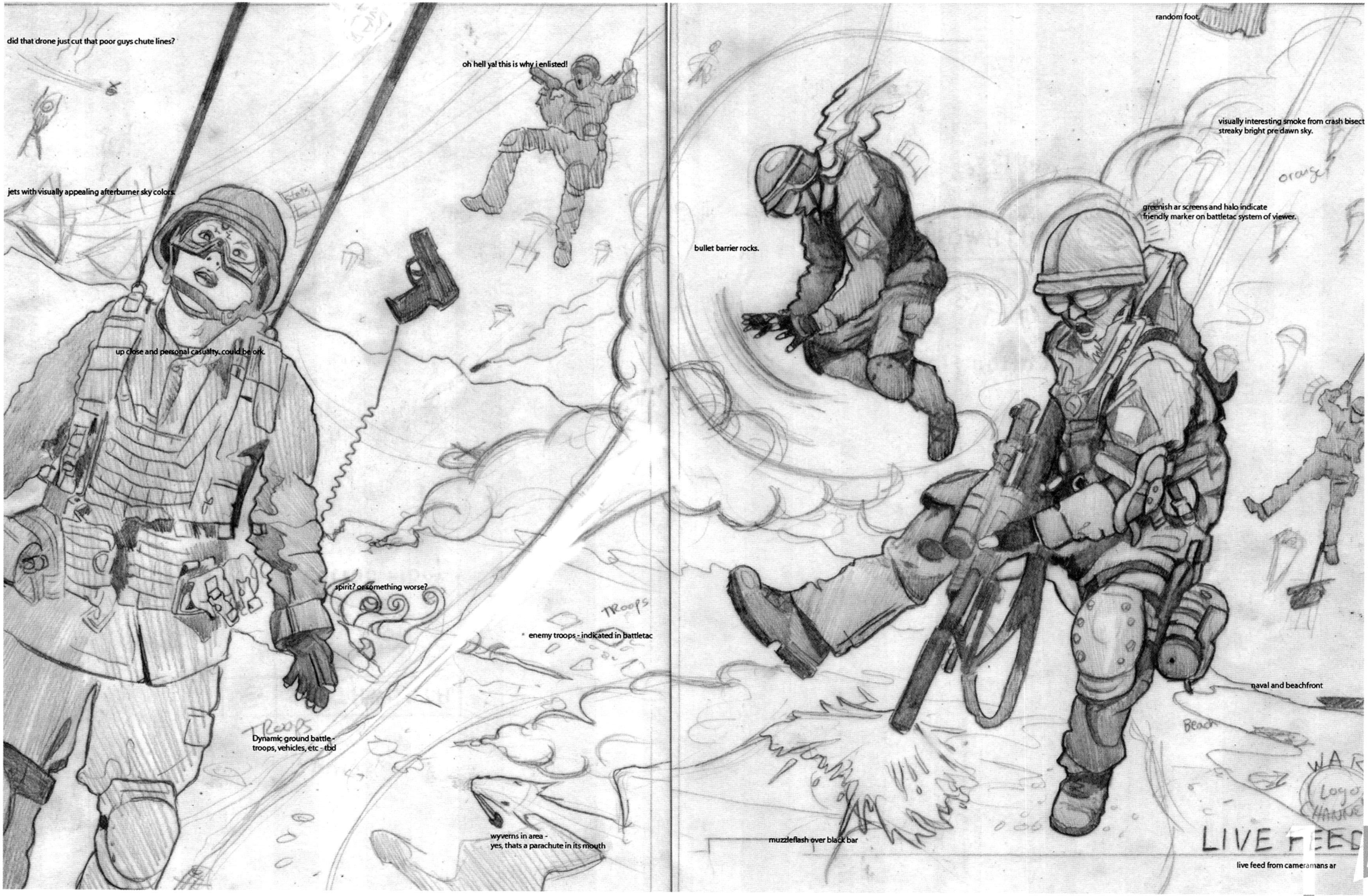
did that drone just cut that poor guys chute lines?
oh hell ya! this is why i enlisted!
jets with visually appealing afterburner sky colors.
up close and personal casualty. could be ork.
spirit? or something worse?
TROOPS
enemy troops - indicated in battletac
TROOPS
Dynamic ground battle -
troops, vehicles, etc - tbd
wyverns in area -
yes, thats a parachute in its mouth
random foot.
visually interesting smoke from crash bisect
streaky bright pre dawn sky.
orange
greenish ar screens and halo indicate
friendly marker on battletac system of viewer.
bullet barrier rocks.
naval and beachfront
Beach
muzzleflash over black bar
LIVE FEED
live feed from cameramans ar

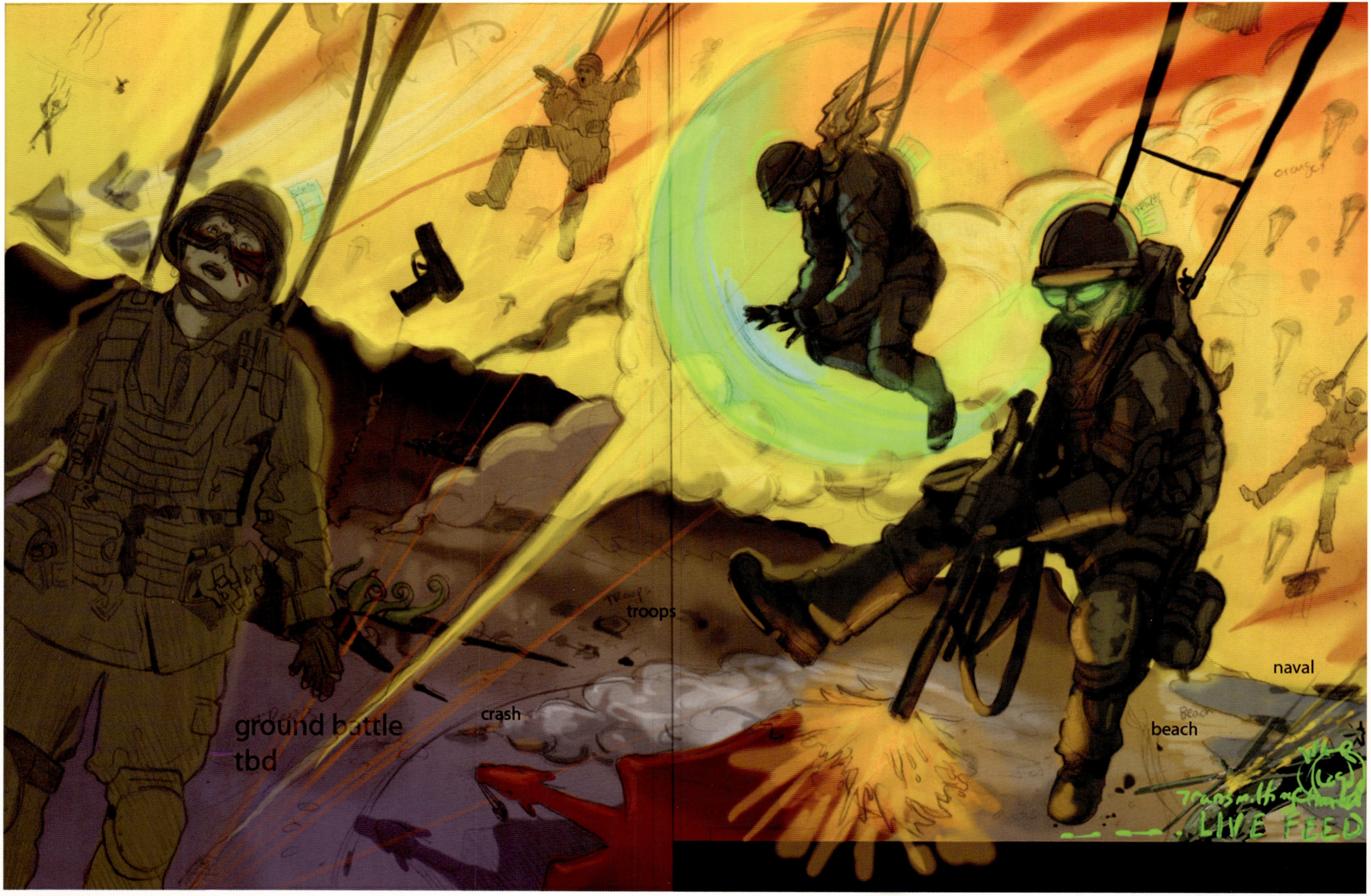
ground battle
tbd
crash
troops
beach
naval
LIVE FEED

WAR!

Initially the direction that I was given was to create an overtly military-themed illustration for the Shadowrun universe about a war in South America. They wanted it to be "very gritty and very military". I spent a lot of time sketching, designing, coordinating model shoots, prepping reference, and producing a color study.

My concept for this piece was a pre-dawn air drop. Well....almost. Technically the concept for this was: "Oh ••••. We missed the pre-dawn and now everyone can see us. We are all going to die. Fubar."

My fellow Shadowrun players and team mates just happen to also participate in Airsoft events and competitions, so had all this amazing military and paramilitary gear. They came over to the studio and we spent the night getting caffeinated and shooting away. In some cases, several men had to stand on chairs to hold up the kits of the model so he could pose as if falling. It was a terrific experience.

Then on the third round of discussion with the art director, everyone realized that there weren't enough Shadowrunners in the art notes (aka, non-professional, non-uniform-wearing, non-affiliated, individuals). I kept the front of the book similar, but re-worked the back. Thankfully, the publisher gave me the time, and I prefer the inconsistent gear of scrounging shadowrunners.

My favorite character in the scene is modelled by Lazarus. He's the one without the parachute. Read into that what you will but he will probably be the only one to survive the drop.

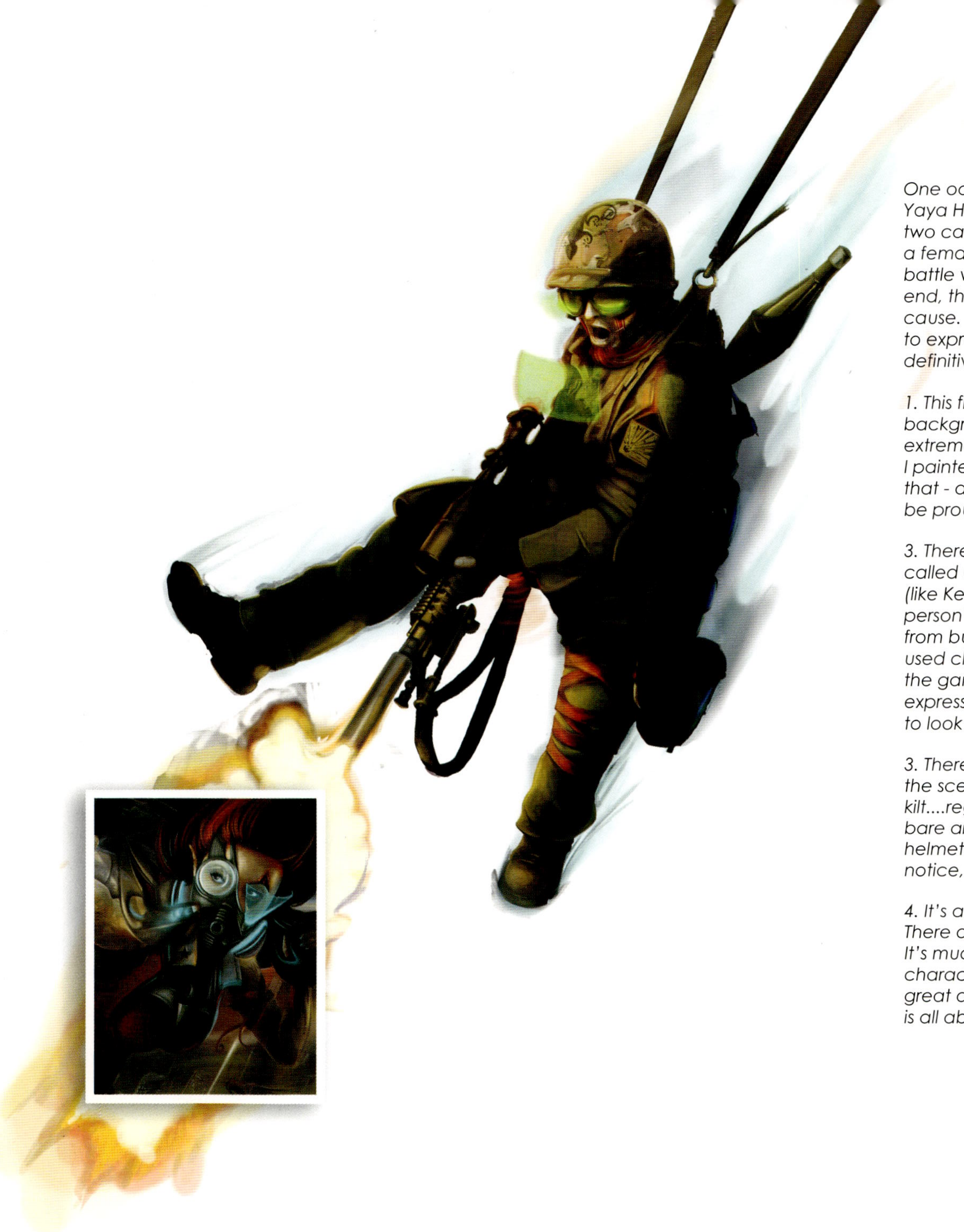

One odd controversy occurred over Yaya Han's cleavage. There were two camps revolving around whether a female warrior would ever go into battle with exposed cleavage. In the end, the prudes won one for their cause. As the artist, I feel it important to express my intent clearly and definitively:

1. This fictional character has a Yakuza background, to whom tattoos are an extremely important part of her culture. I painted tattoos on her to because of that - and those tattoos would have to be proudly displayed in battle.

3. There is a product in Shadowrun called Orthoskin™. It is a synthetic fiber (like Kevlar™) that is woven through a person's skin, giving them protection from bullets and knives. It's a commonly used character enhancement in the game and one that players use expressly for allowing their characters to look cool while being dangerous.

3. There is also a man wearing a kilt in the scene and he's parachuting....In a kilt....regimental, no doubt. The Troll has bare arms. The orc wears jeans and no helmet. The only one that ever gets any notice, however, is the woman.

4. It's a fantasy illustration. Not reality. There are dragons in the same picture, It's much more fun to look at cool, sexy characters of both genders with really great affectations. That's what gaming is all about!

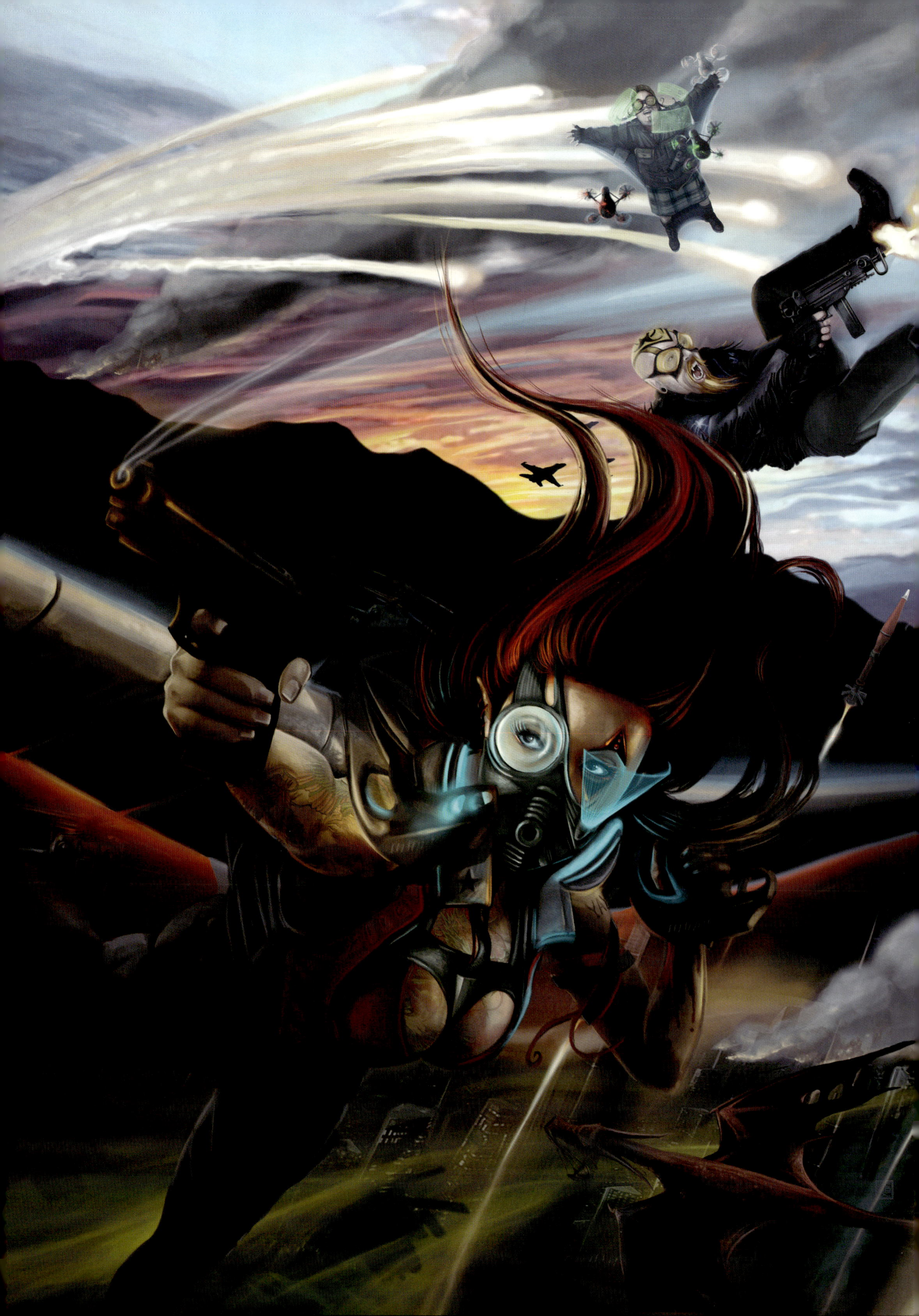

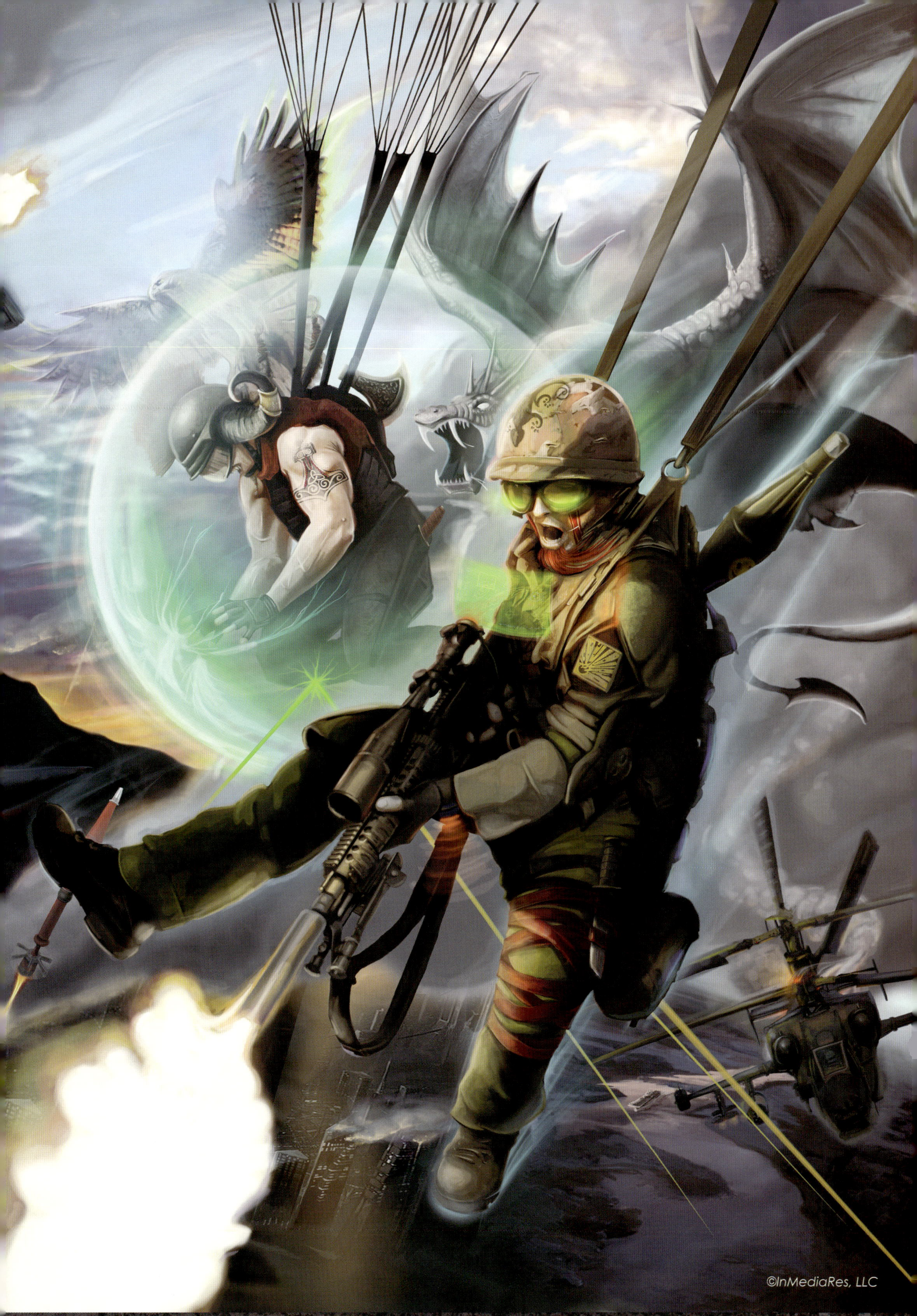

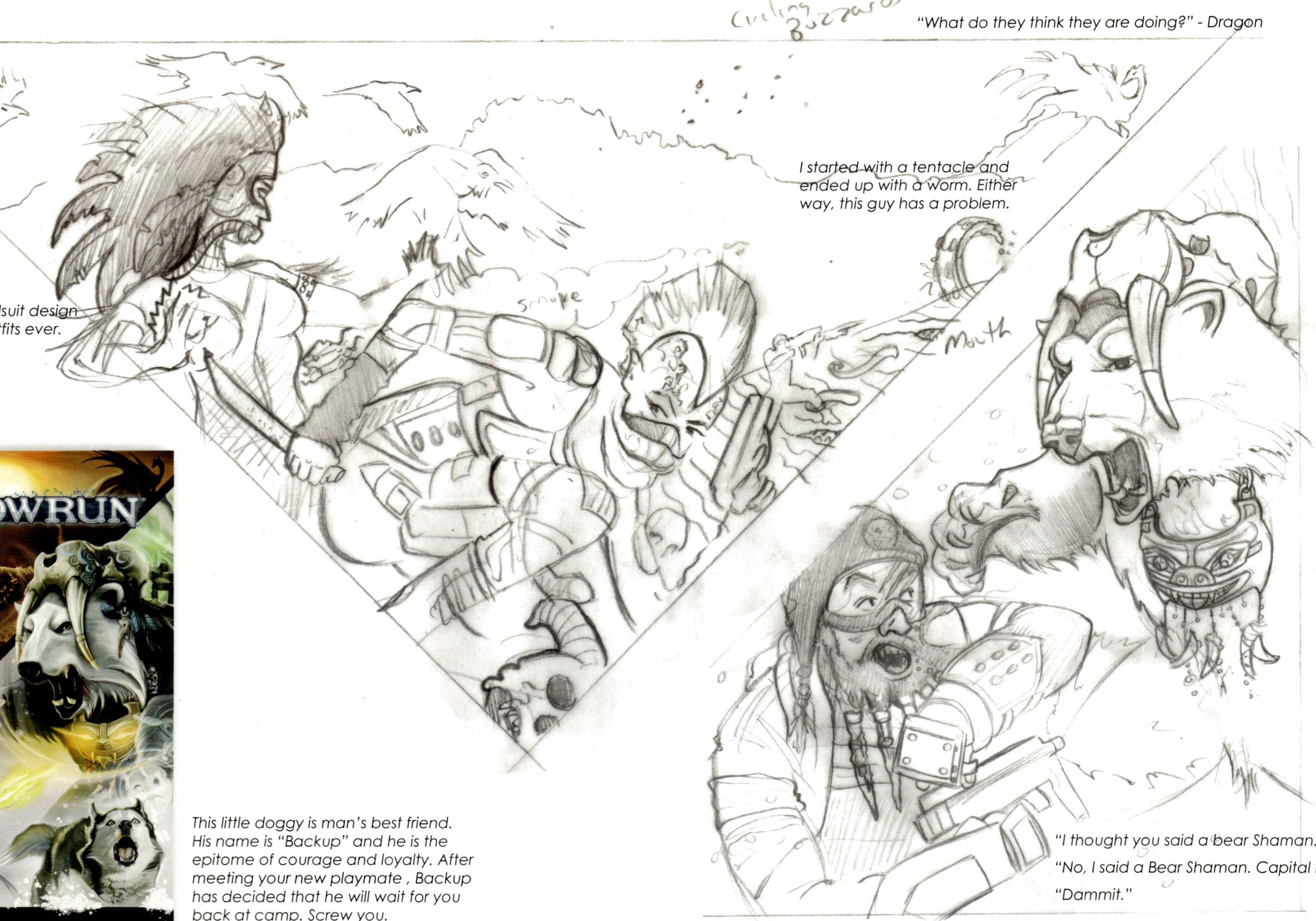

"What do they think they are doing?" - Dragon

I started with a tentacle and ended up with a worm. Either way, this guy has a problem.

The Raven shaman's stillsuit design is one of my favorite outfits ever. Shadowrun a la Dune.

"I thought you said a bear Shaman."

"No, I said a Bear Shaman. Capital B."

"Dammit."

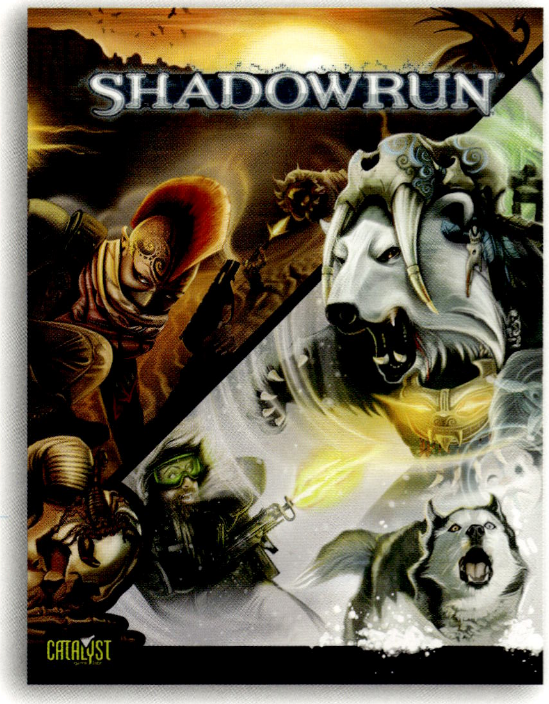

This little doggy is man's best friend. His name is "Backup" and he is the epitome of courage and loyalty. After meeting your new playmate , Backup has decided that he will wait for you back at camp. Screw you.

Hazard Pay

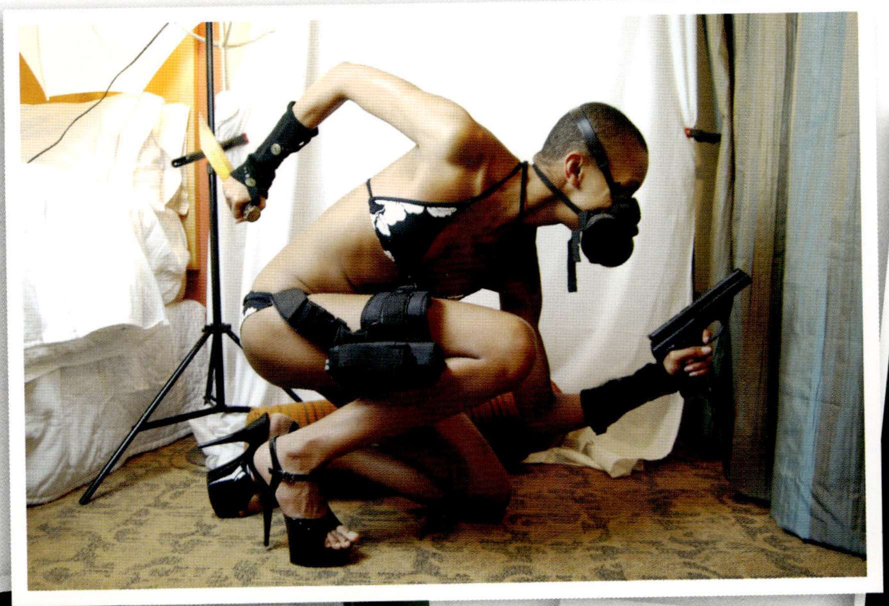

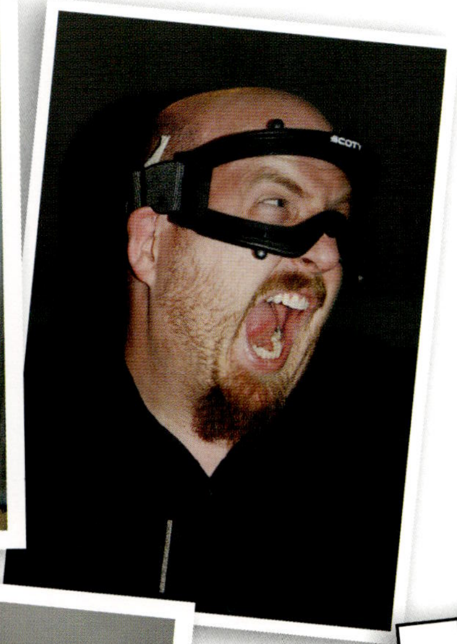

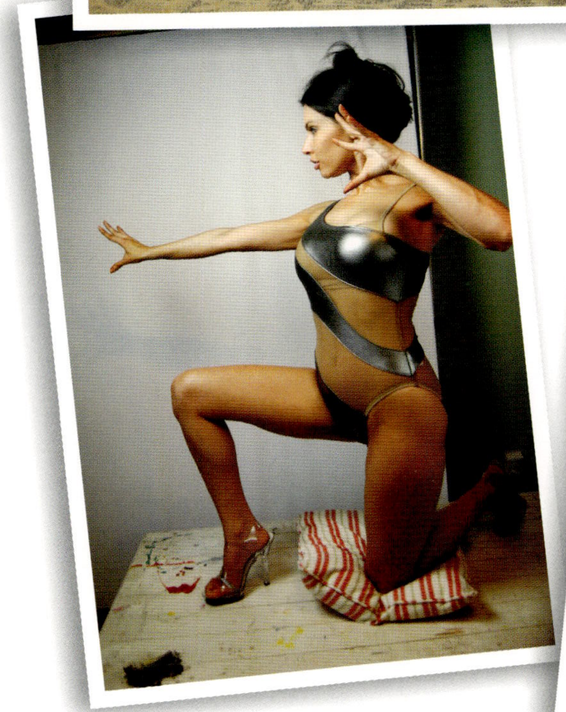

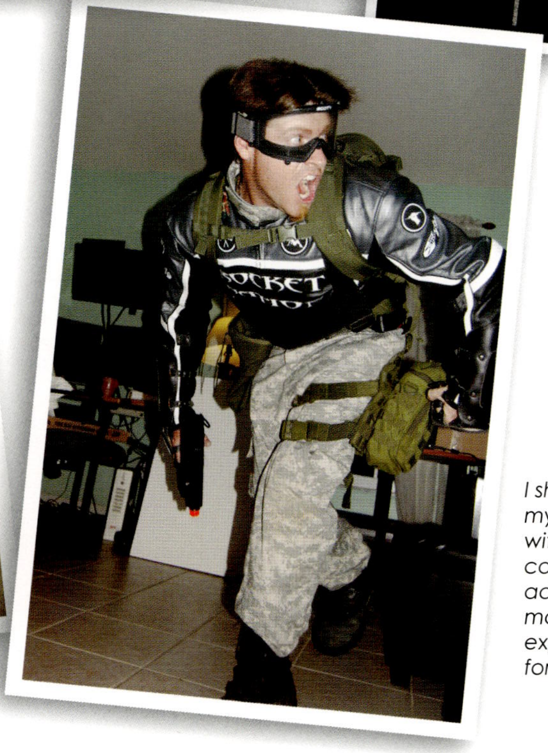

I shoot a lot of my reference without the exact costuming, and add it later. I'm mostly looking for expression and form.

Every once in a while, the art notes will ask for something really tricky. They have a concept in mind that they are certain will work, but I propose a visually better solution. It is times like these that it helps to have an art director who believes in you enough to follow your vision.

Hazard Pay was offered to me as a cover requiring three separate illustrations of Desert, Arctic, and Space - combined into one cover. There were a number of creative challenges with this. If I divided it horizontally - the top third would be covered by type. If I chose three vertical layouts there would be an odd truncation on the spine, leaving portions on the back and front of the book. So I created a unique triangular layout.

The "center' illustration of the desert is really two scenes, one for the front and one of the back. The arctic scene provided enough distance and dichotomy from the desert to get the message that the book was about a large range of circumstances.

I love the speed differences of the action in the three panels and the mixed uniforms in the space scene. This book is about overly dangerous situations - so I included a lot of foreboding elements - the circling vultures, the impending dragon, and the skull on the front pointing in the same direction as the characters.

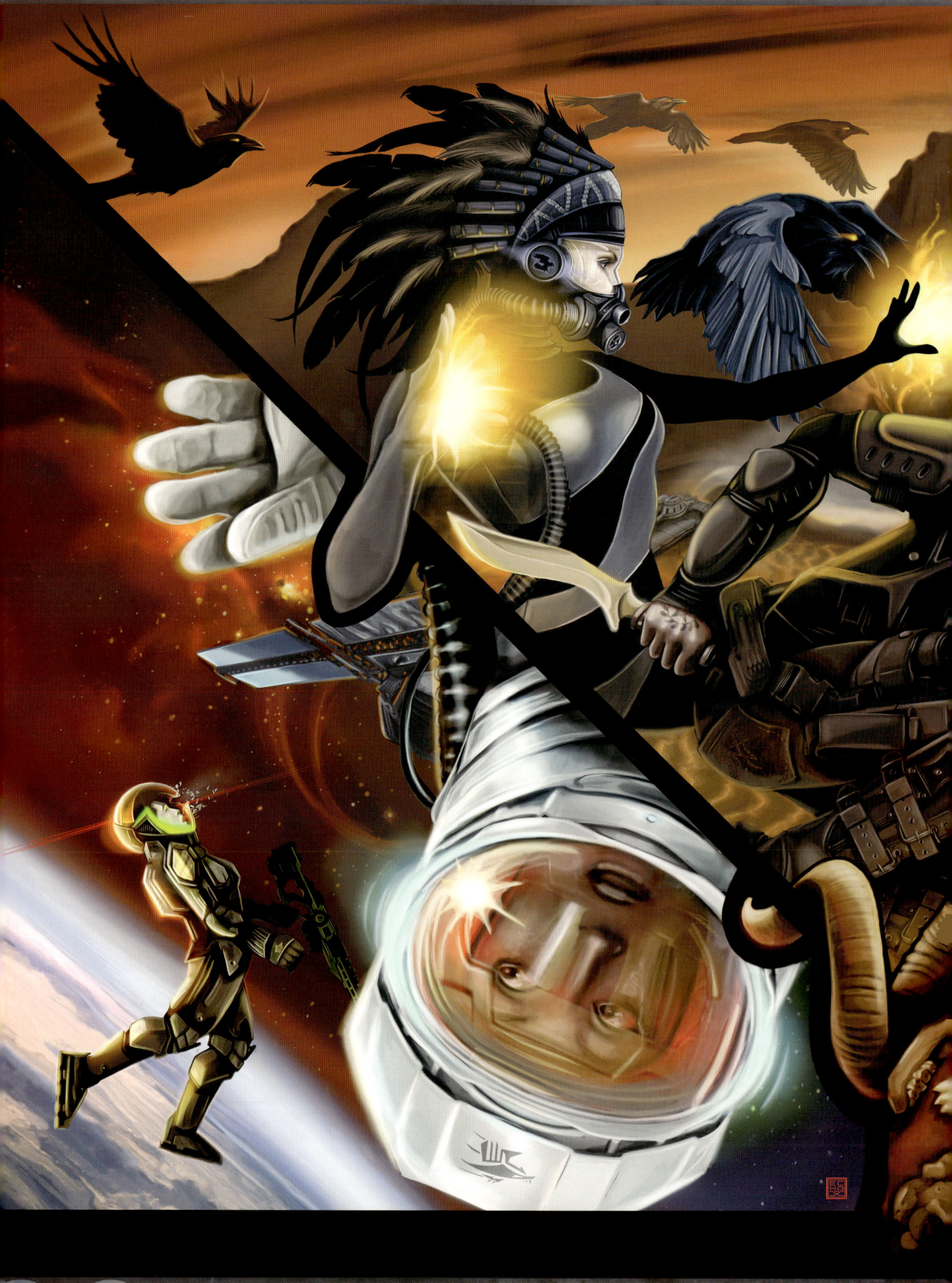

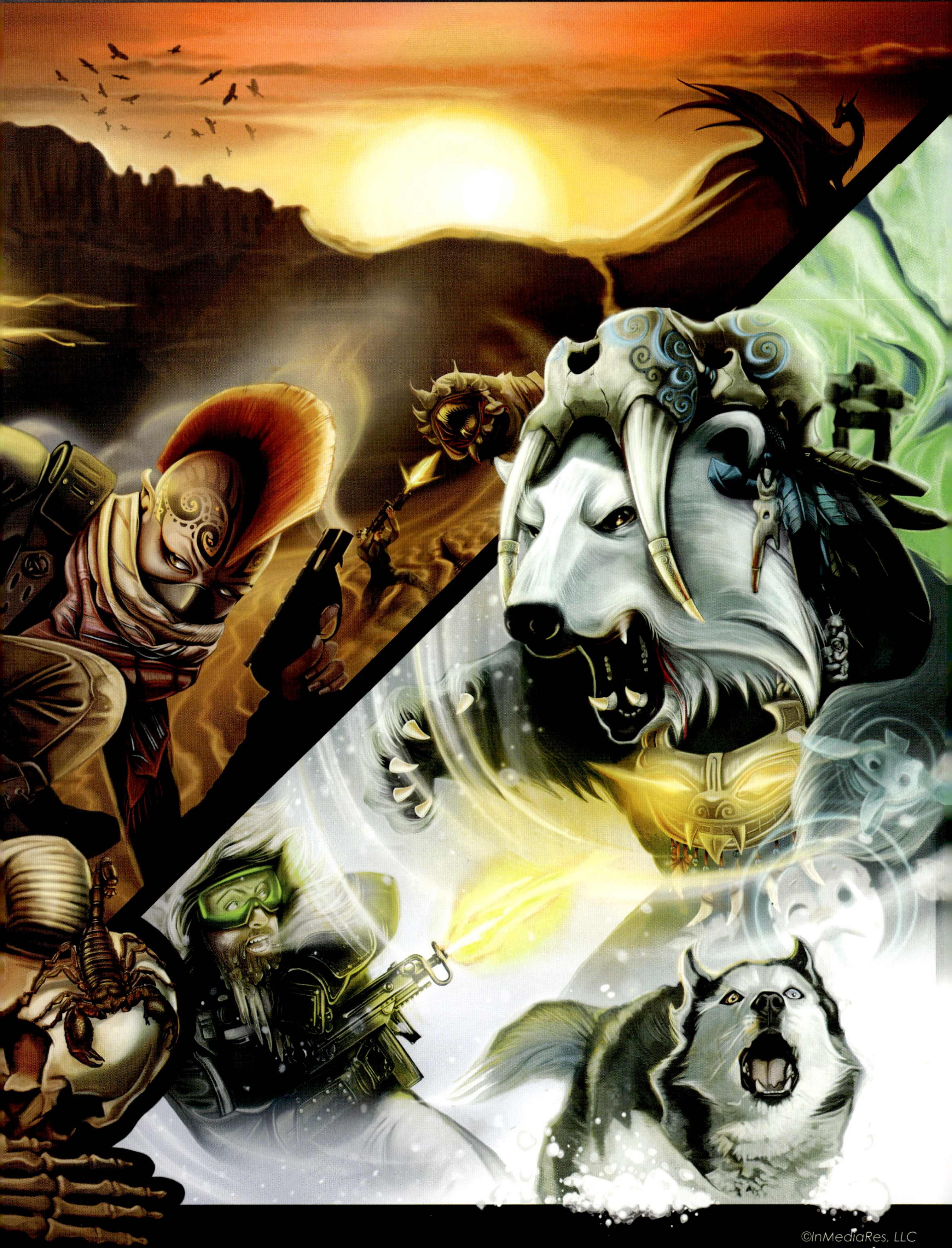

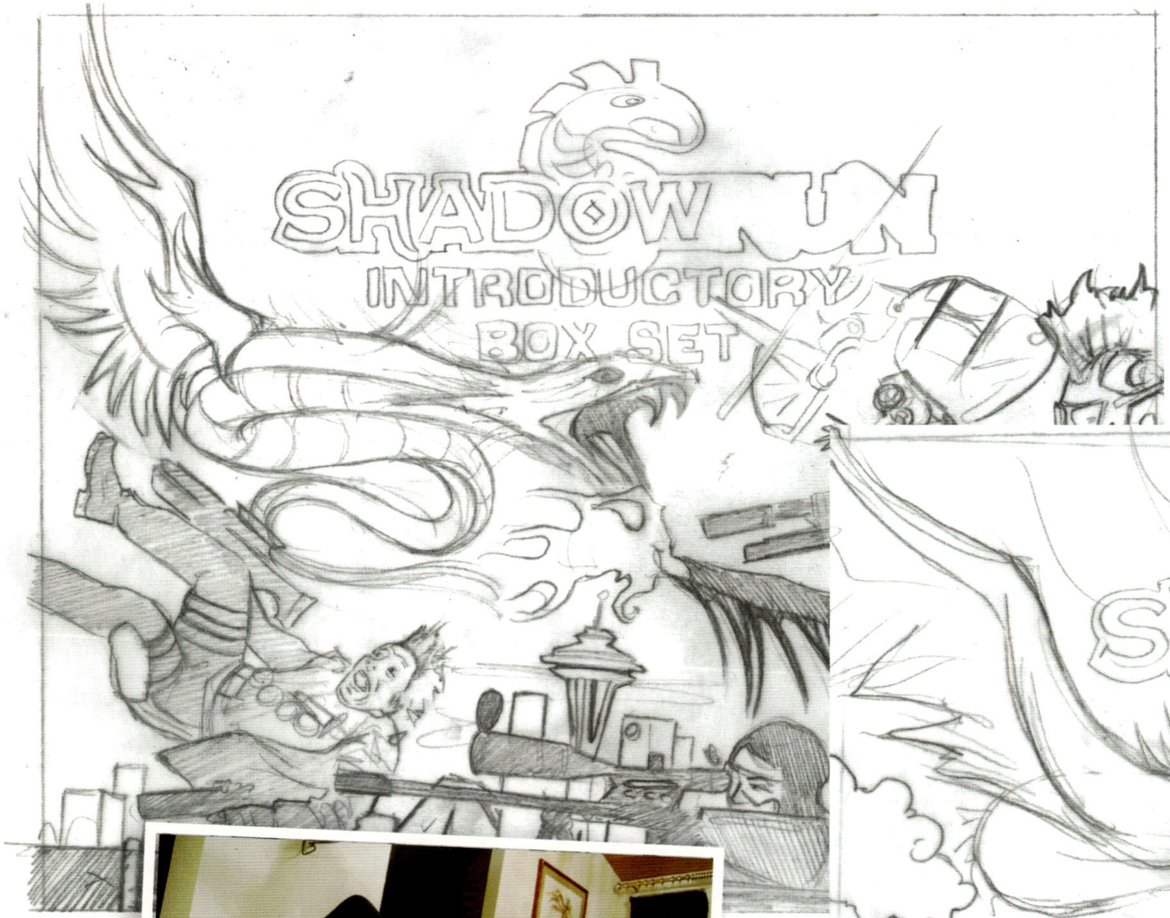

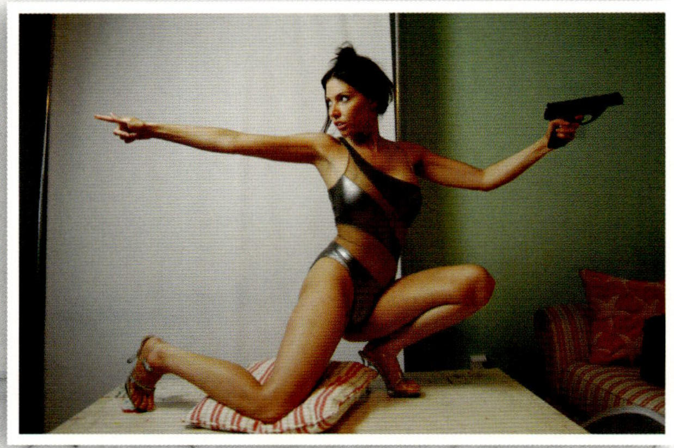

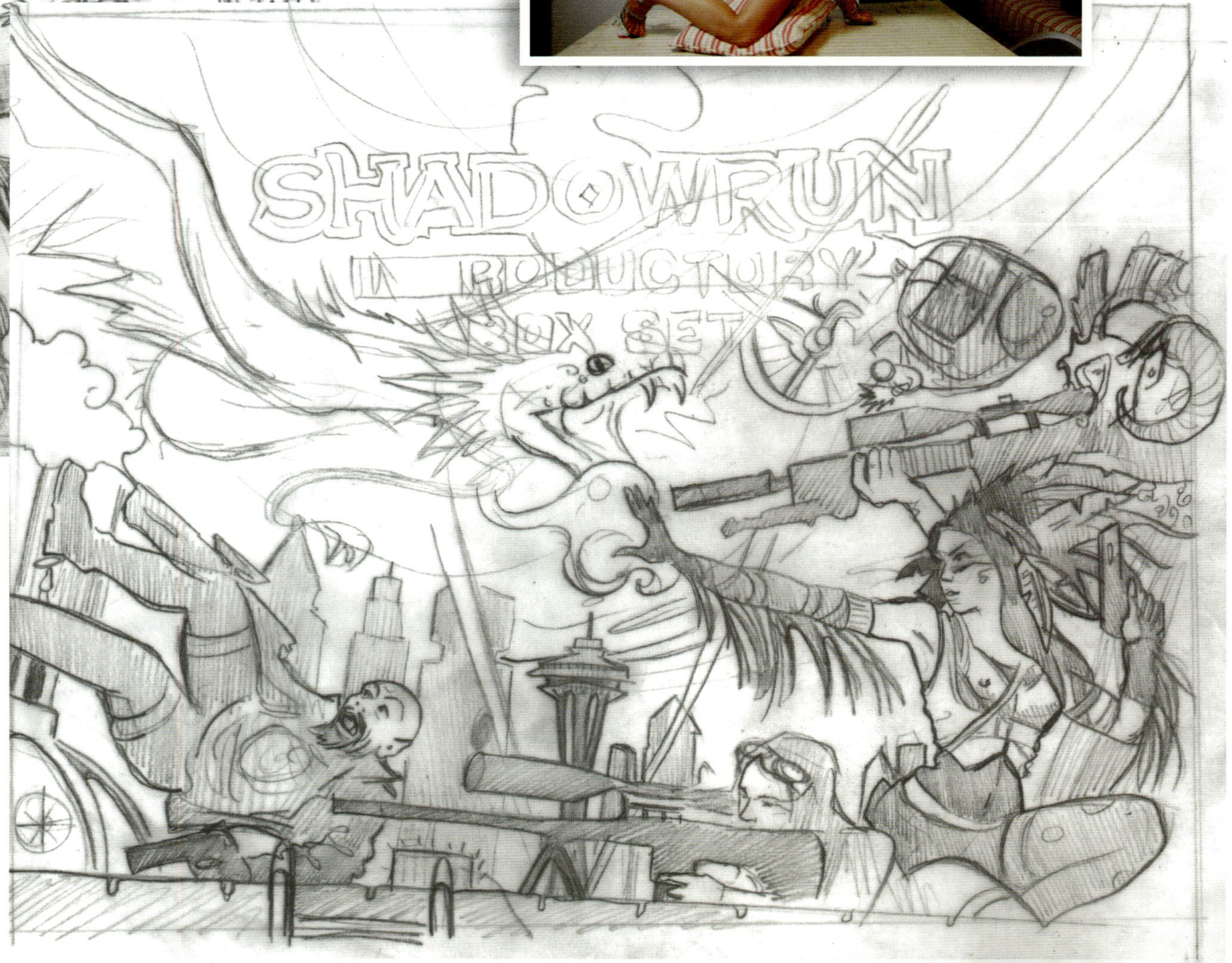

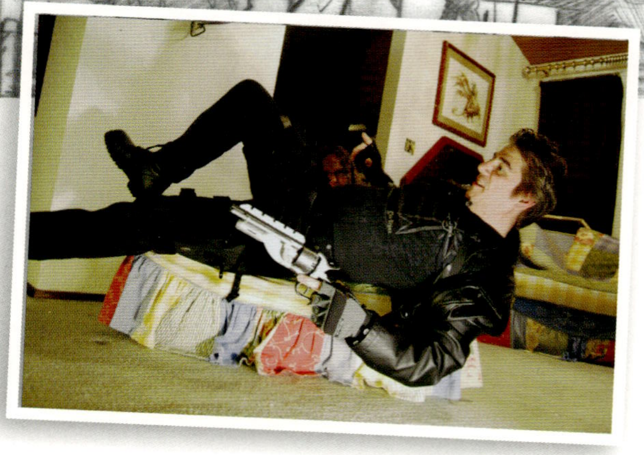

Hey Chris, why don't you come over tonight and let us throw grenades at you? Just leap backwards in a panic and shoot back at us, if you can.

Introductory Box Set

I'd had a roof-top extraction scene in my mind for months, when this project dropped in my lap. Unfortunately for me, I was imagining a vertical book cover, and this landscape box did not fit my original vision. So the concept had to evolve.

The Seattle rooftop battle sketch was approved immediately. The art director just asked me to conform to some of the same characters from the cover of Shadowrun 5 main source book and to make the sky reddish (the original pitch was greenish).

Instead of showing both the anti-heroes and the semi-villains engaged, I chose an escape scene rendezvousing with the team's re-purposed DocWagon helicopter. Since the SR5 cover featured a large spirit, I decided that the box cover needed a dragon. Specifically, I chose to depict a feathered serpent in hazy toxic skies (to the chagrin of the chopper pilot).

My version of the Shadowrun universe is perpetually gritty. I enjoy the dichotomy of the slick corporate world with the dark corners of the streets. I like my characters to look pieced together, with mismatched uniforms and hints to their pasts. I love leaving the streets littered with shell casings of battles gone by, a random bloody handprint on a wall, bits of graffiti, and omens of foreboding. In my vision, these are all reminders that this is a moment beyond the present. This is a world with a past and possibly a future. It is a universe unto itself with countless stories that have happened or are yet to come.

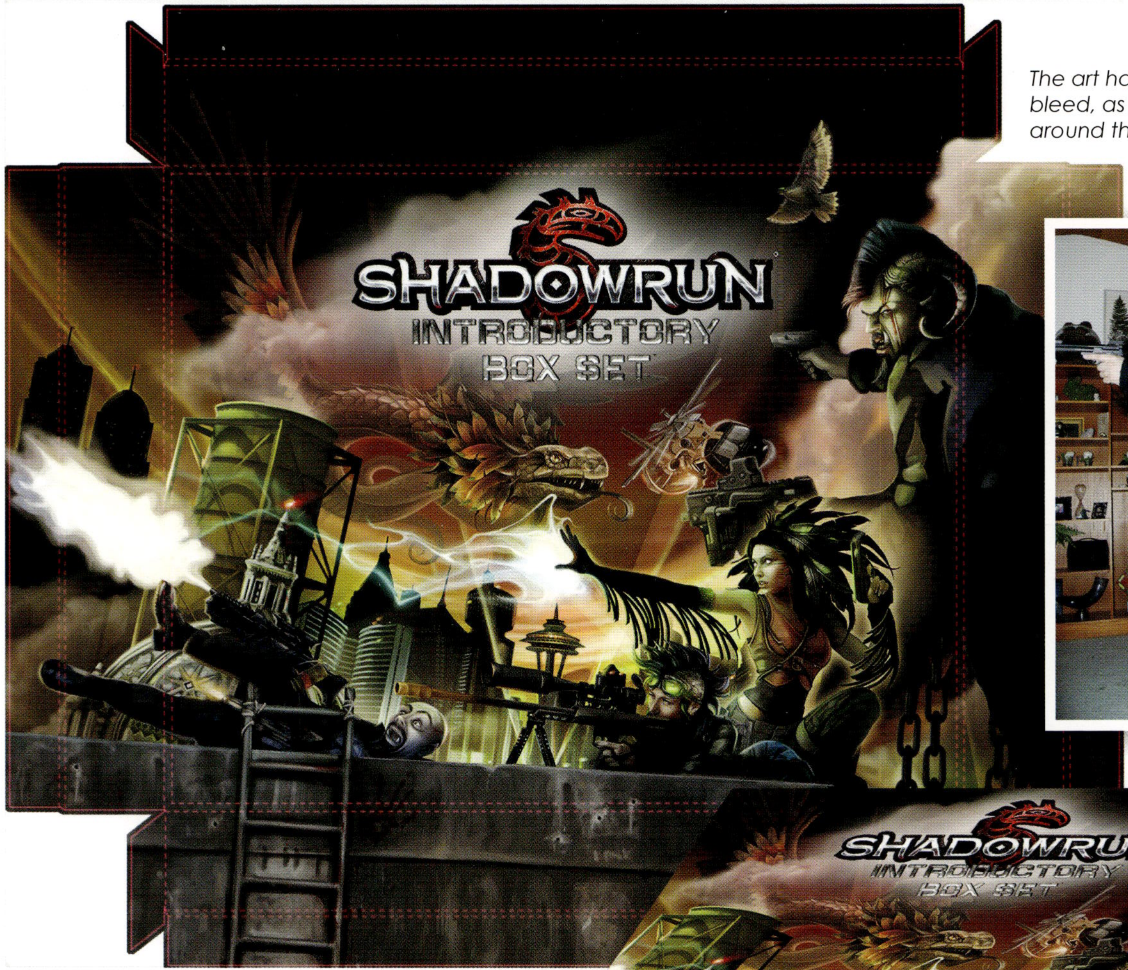

The art has a tremendous amount of bleed, as it is designed to wrap around the four sides of the box.

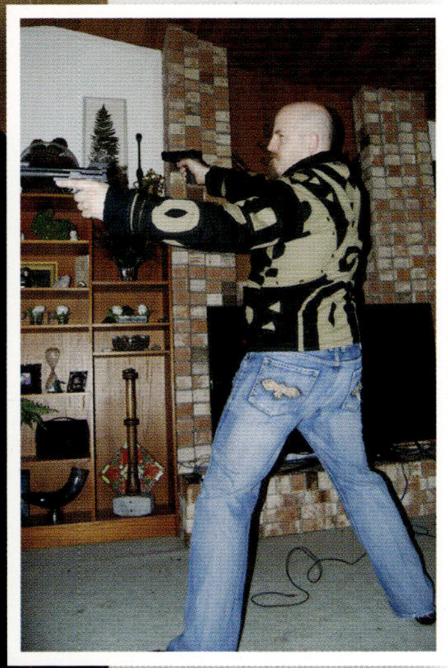

Lazarus trolling-out

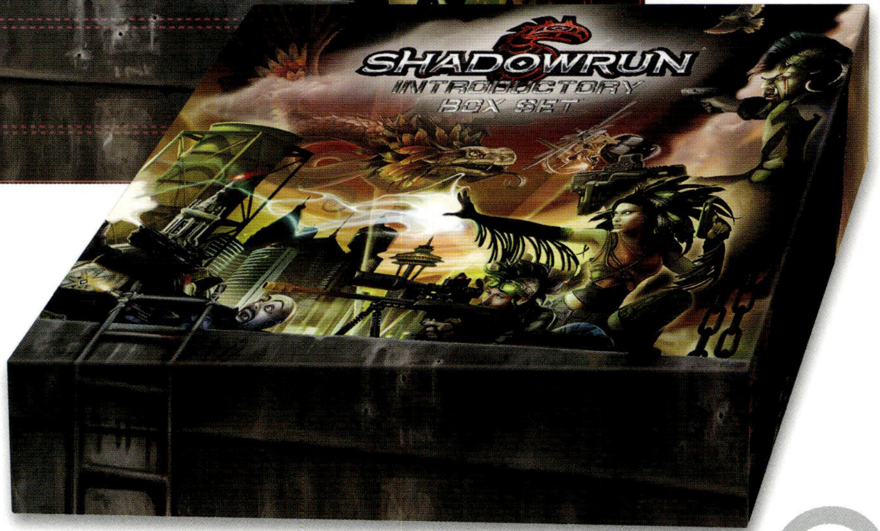

The Mayan Kukulkan and Aztec Quetzalcoatl are ancient dragons with great cultural importance to both cultures. There are countless depictions of them in stone all over Mesoamerica. I researched them in depth and used the original art for inspiration.

I had to leave room for the logo in the upper-center of the piece. Without the logo, the illustration looks low, but with it the box comes alive. (Actual box might vary from this mock-up.)

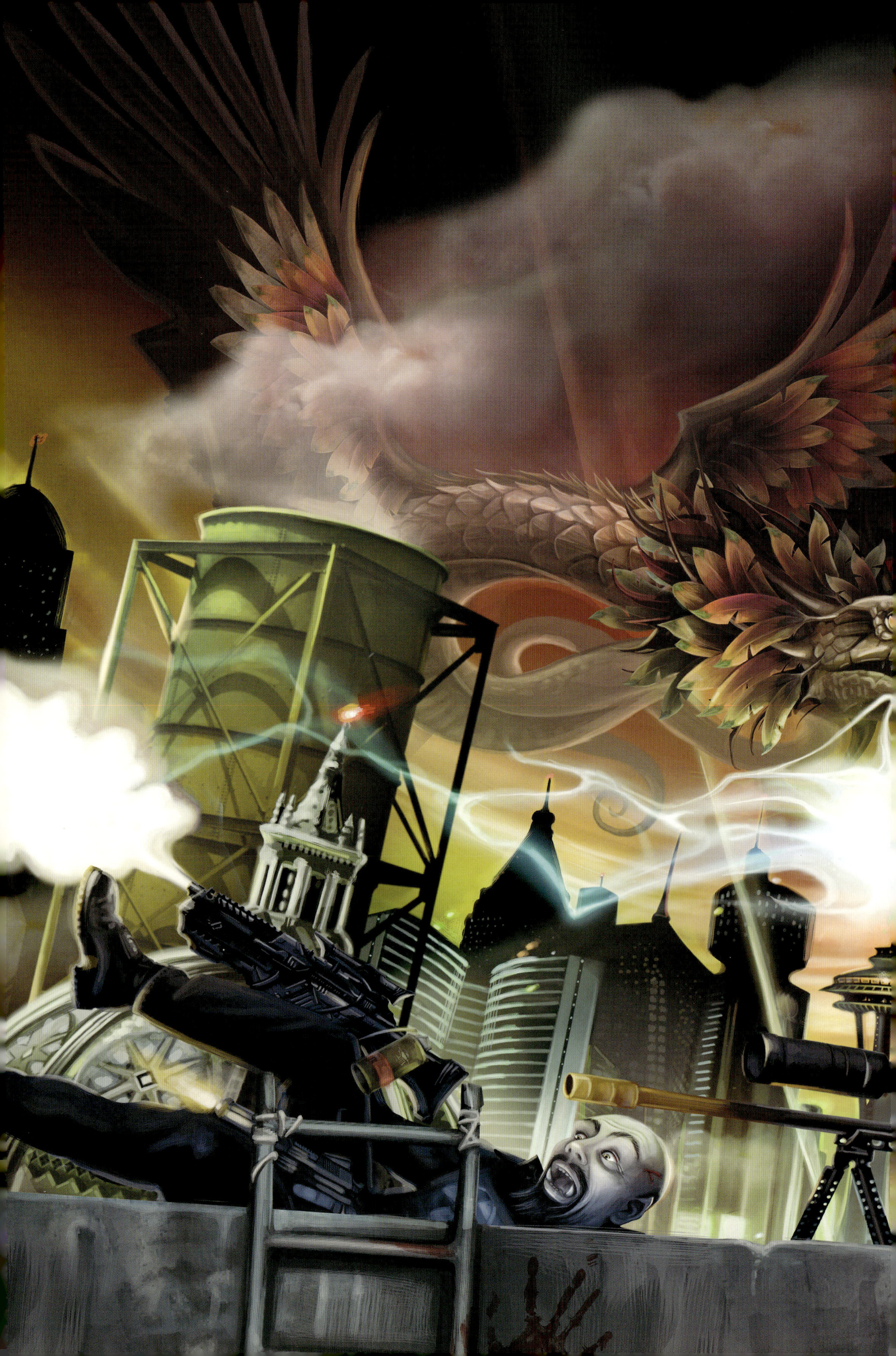

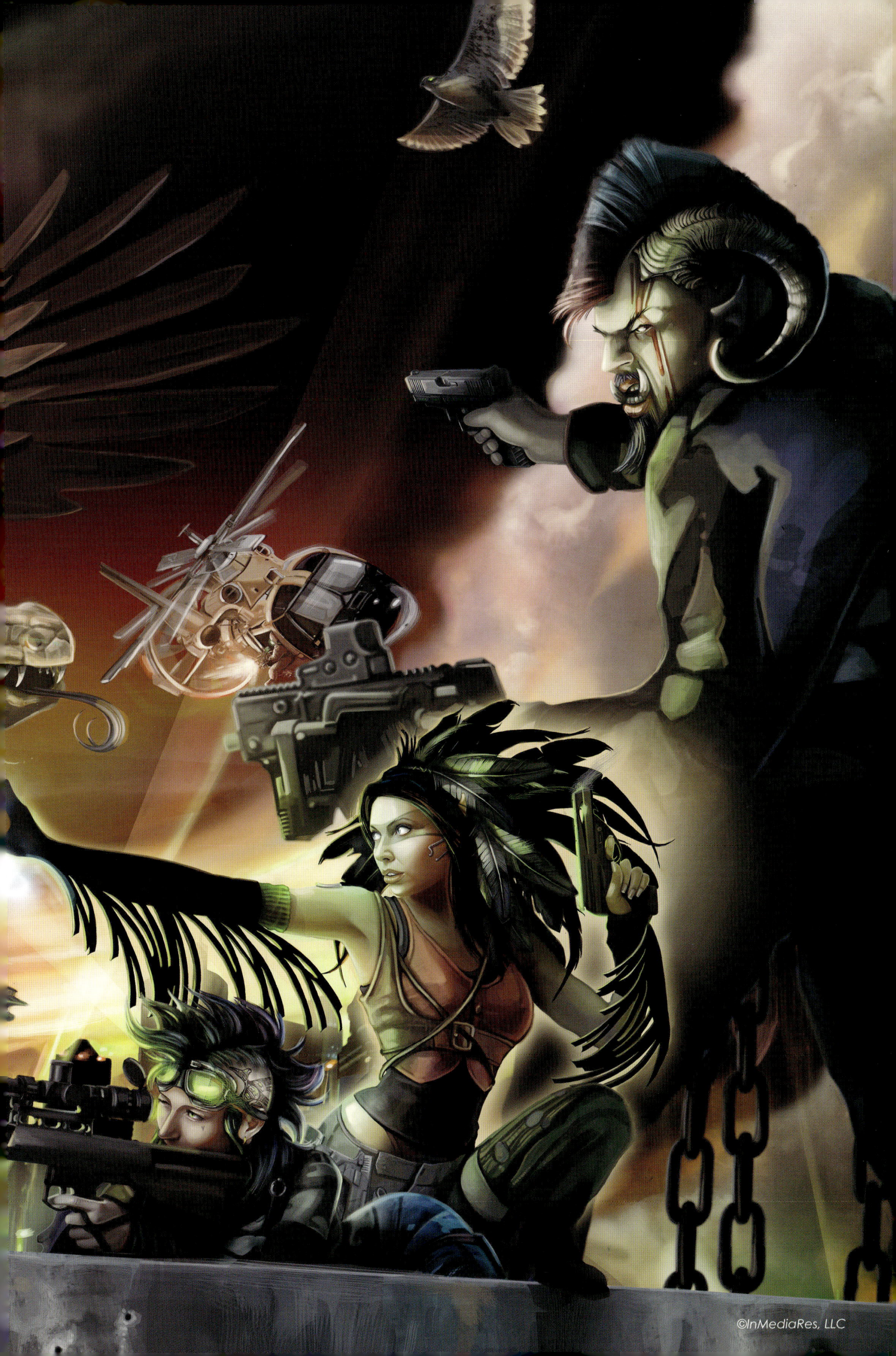

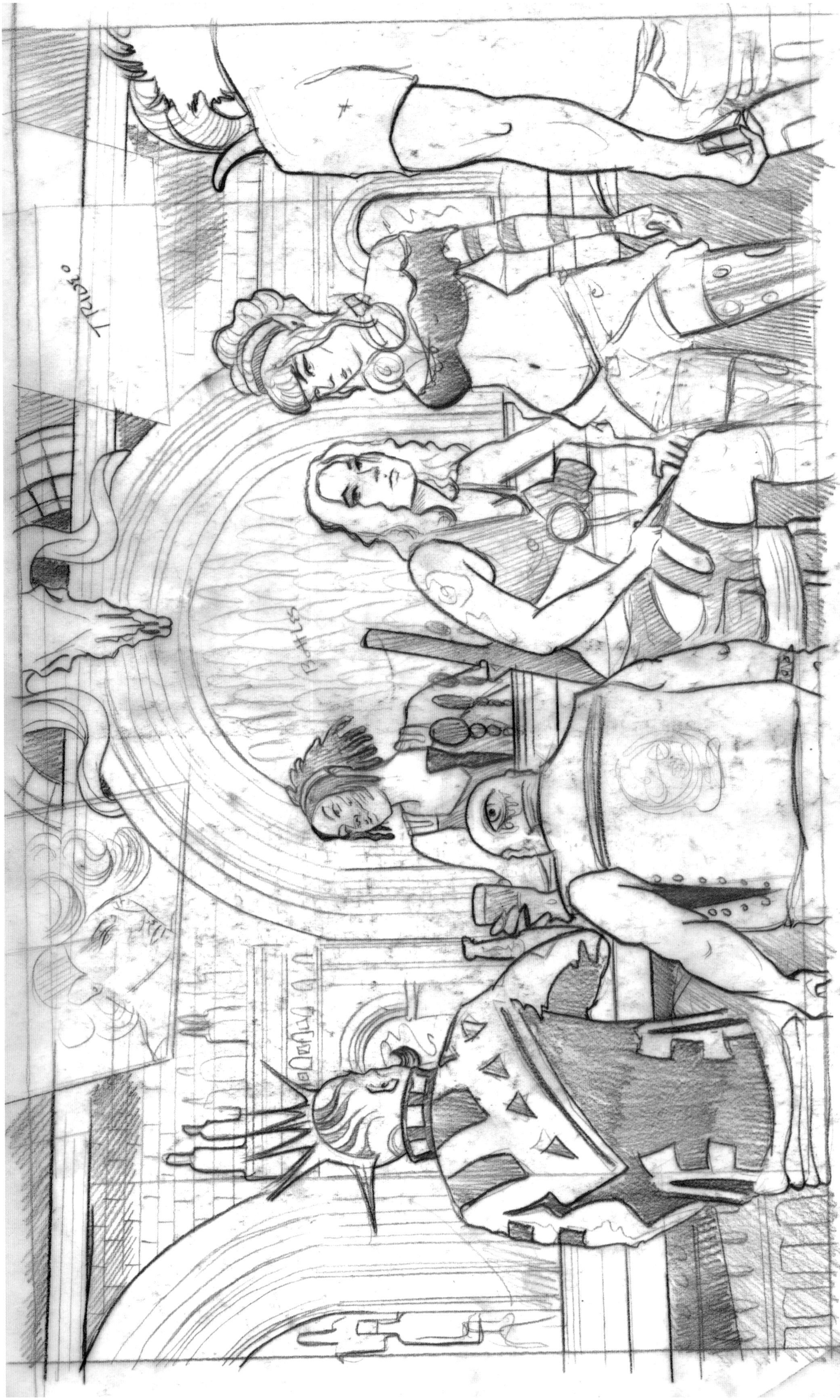

Shadowrun Returns

Shadowrun Returns is a long awaited video game that is a significant update of the classic 1992 game for Sega. It was produced by Harebrained Schemes, spearheaded by one of the original creators of the Shadowrun universe, Jordan Weisman.

This piece is a cover for a collector's edition of an anthology of Shadowrun Returns' game and concept art. The stories within the book center around a certain bar with a lot of history called the Seamstresses Union. While the game version of the bar is lower resolution, we really wanted to capture a more realistic atmosphere of this unique watering hole, which is a central gathering point of many of their characters.

I was supplied concept renderings and text descriptions of the specific characters that they wanted to see included in the scene. Since I use real models to get realistic results, I was quite fortunate to have already shot a few models that matched their concepts so well. With a little bit of artistic magic, I was able to transform digitally created game characters into realistic people with personality within the atmosphere of the bar.

The bar contains the usual suspects, with some going about their business or leisure. On the right, the viewer appears to have stumbled upon or interrupted a conversation. Two of the characters, who were obviously talking about something important, look up. They pause, waiting for you to say or do something... Better make it count.

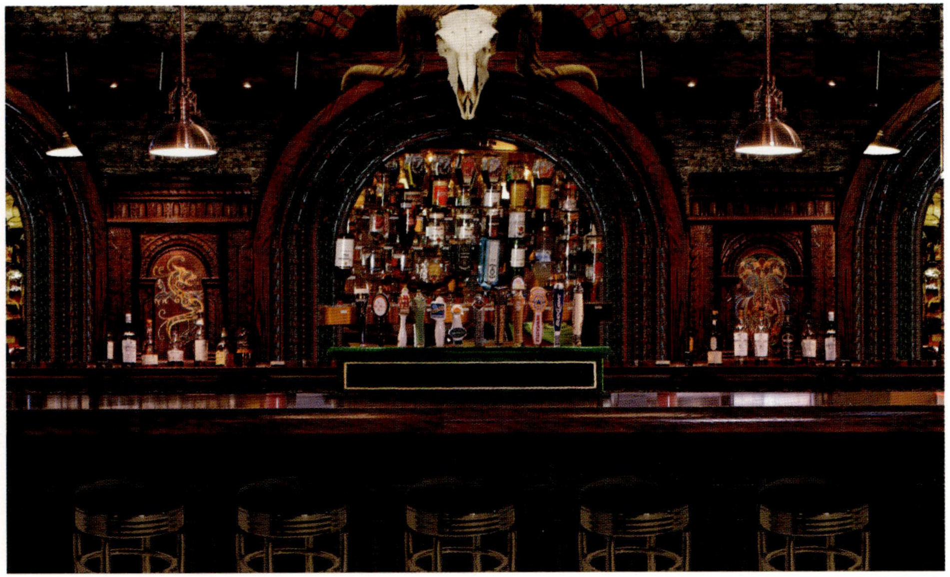

Harebrained Schemes met with me, and showed me the low resolution video game layout of the bar. While keeping the structure true, I photocomposed together a scene (above) that captures the rich depth and detail of an old establishment. Using my mock up, I then adjusted the perspective and added the characters and lighting.

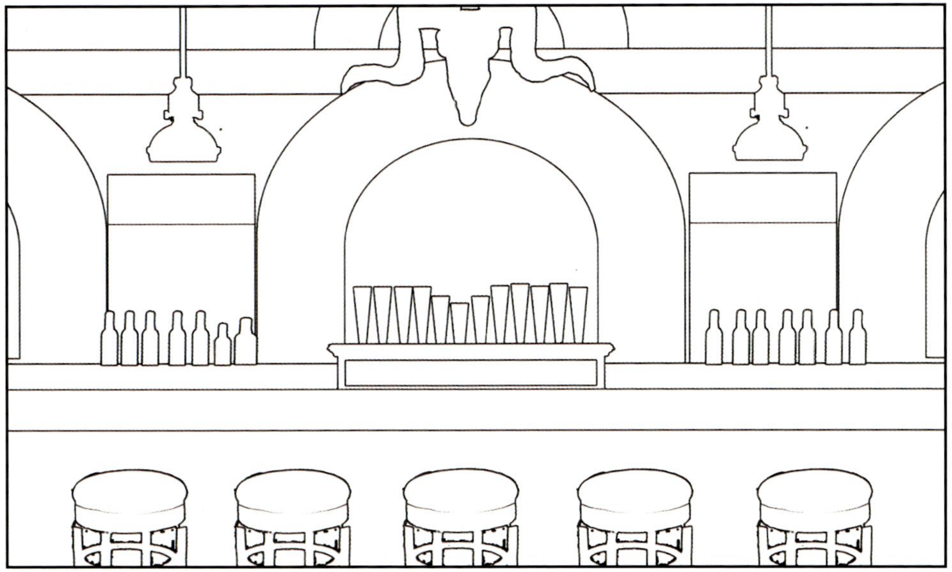

This diagram shows how the many different photos were combined into the final comp for my painting. Each outline represents the placement of a unique photo.

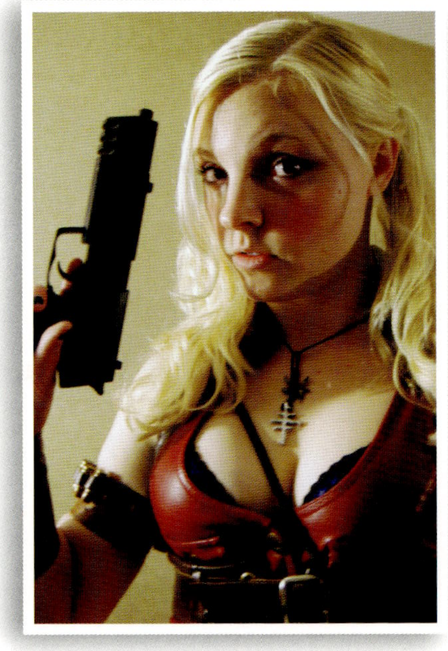

Megan and Angela

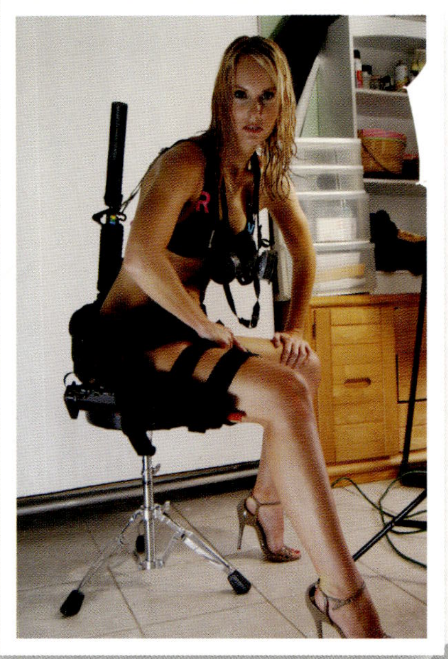

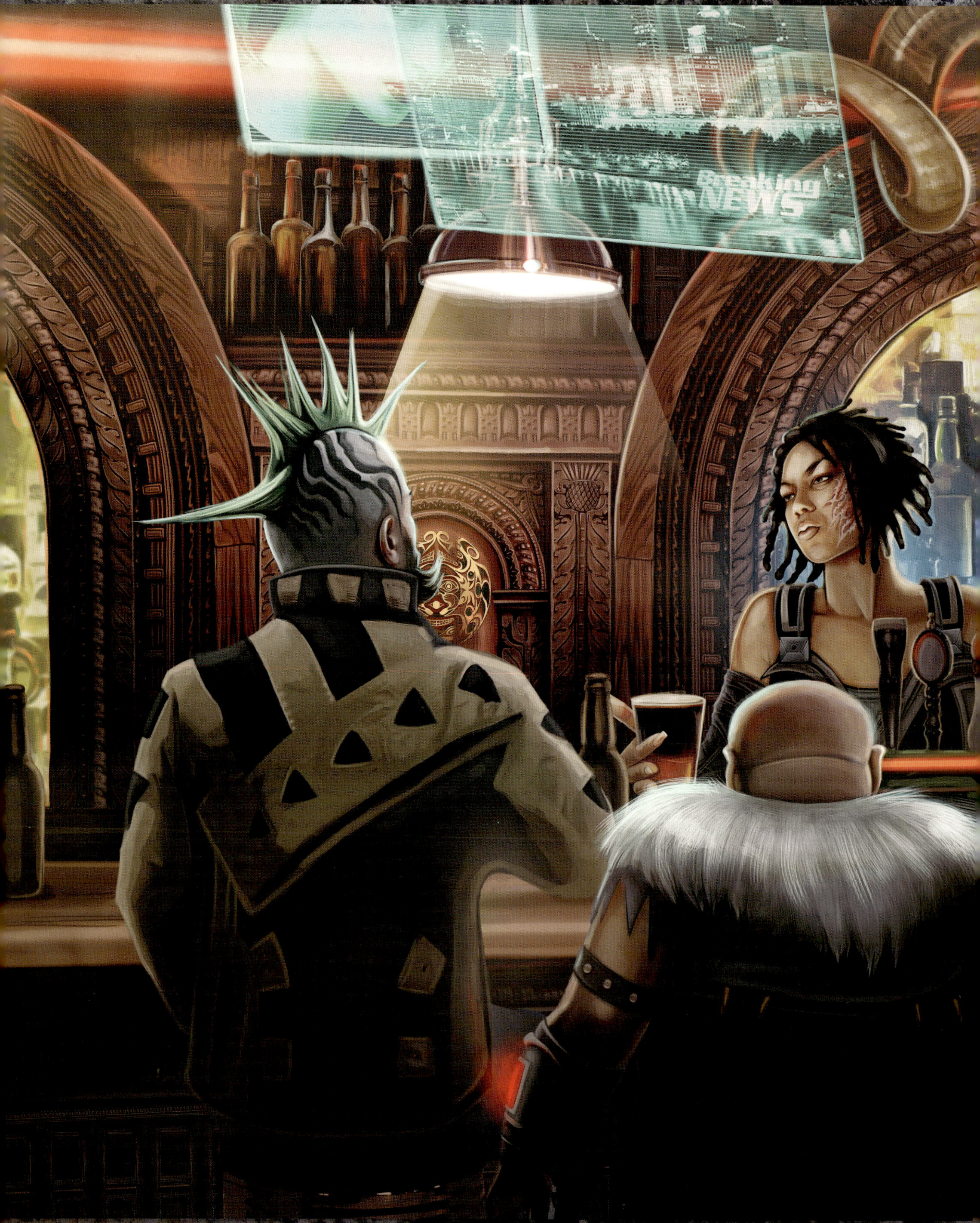
Breaking
NEWS

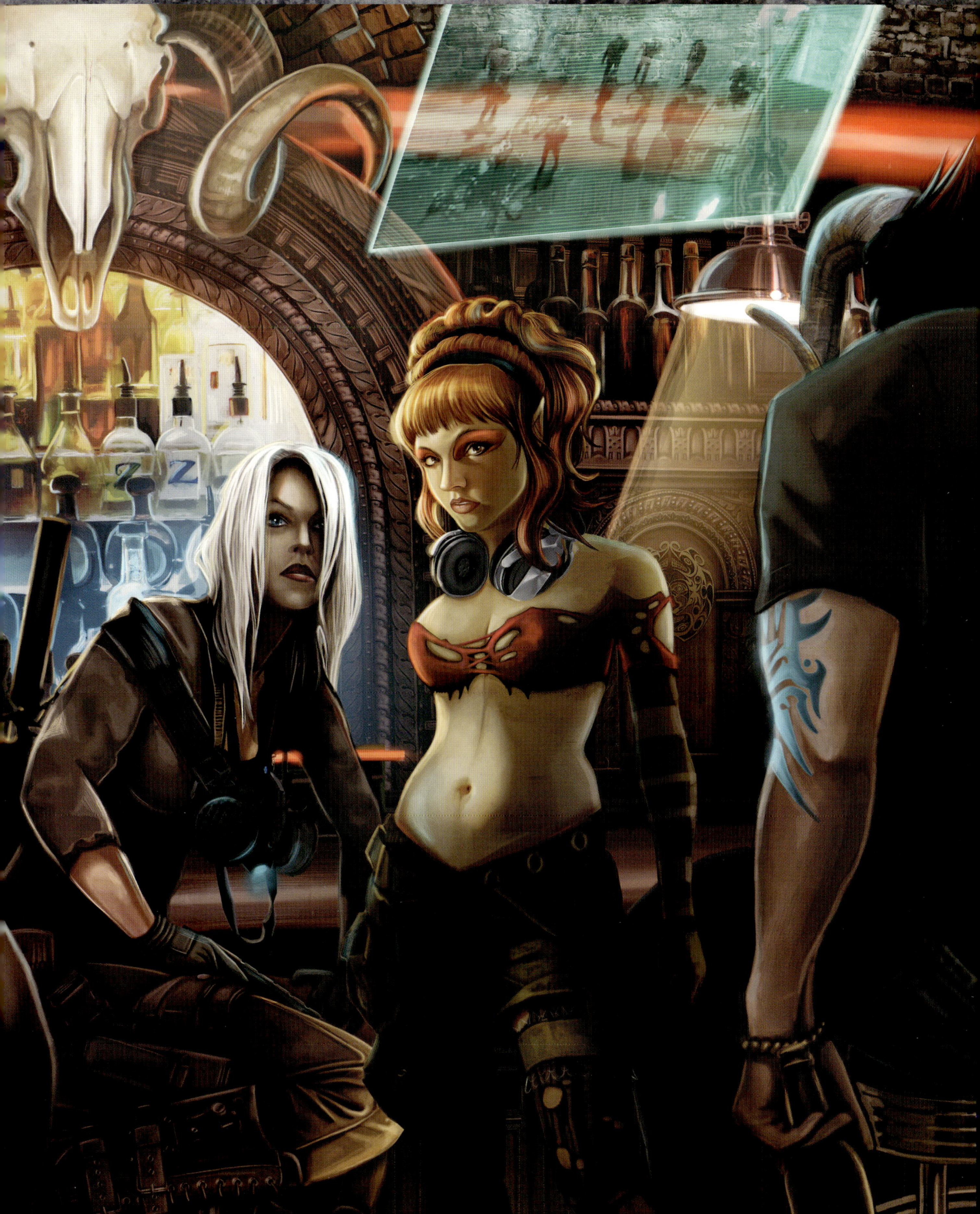

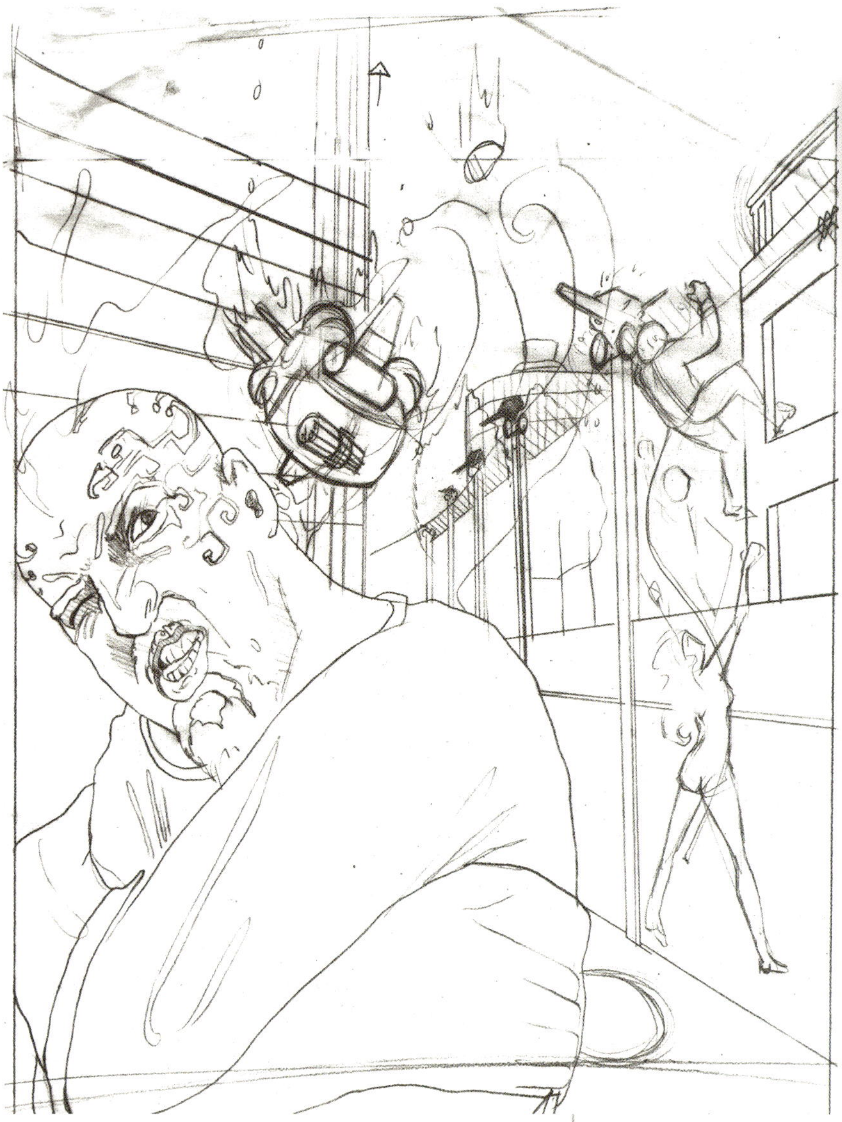

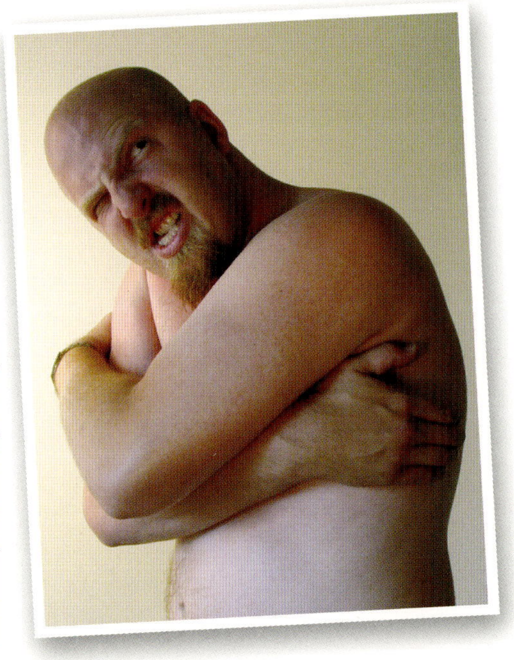

Lazarus meditating.

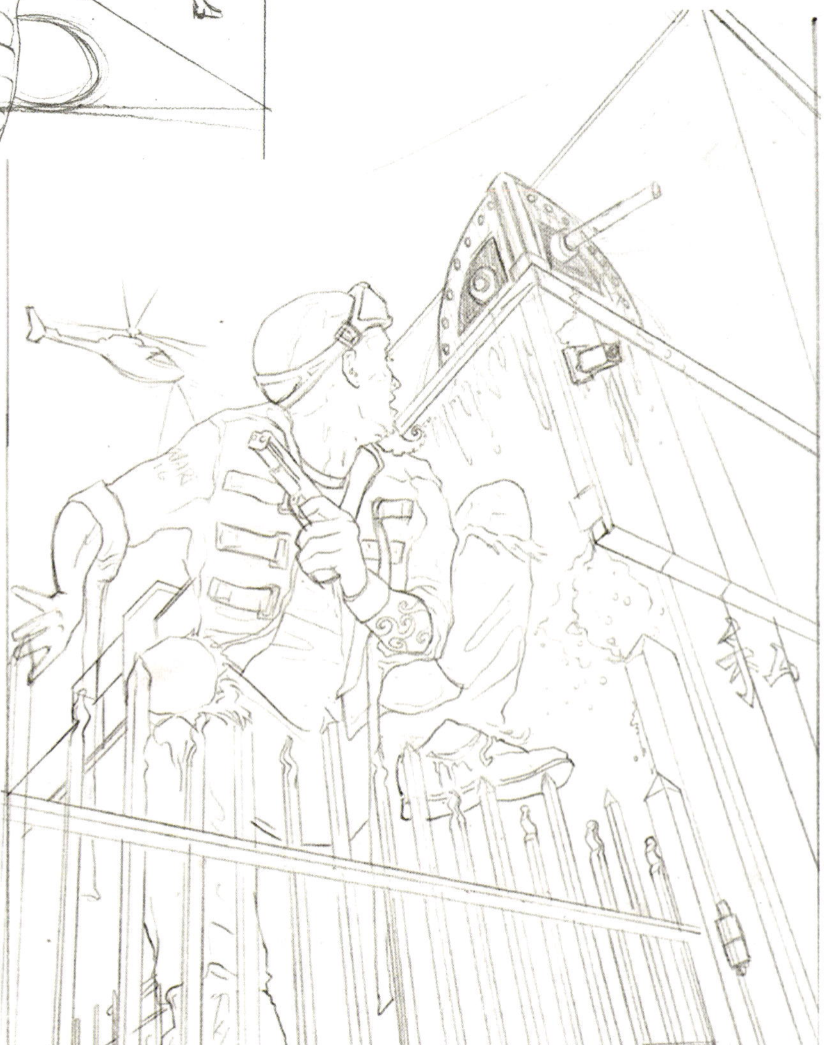

Emergence

I started playing Shadowrun in 1993 with Lazarus, and we play to this day. I received my first rpg game art assignment in 1994, and worked heavily in the game industry for the next five years. However, I was never lucky enough to receive any assignments for the actual game which I played regularly.

Then I moved on to advance my career and soon became a top advertising illustrator with major retail and packaging clients, all the while keeping game art in my heart. Eventually the time came when I randomly sent an inquiry to Catalyst 'just for fun'. They surprised me the assignment for Emergence.

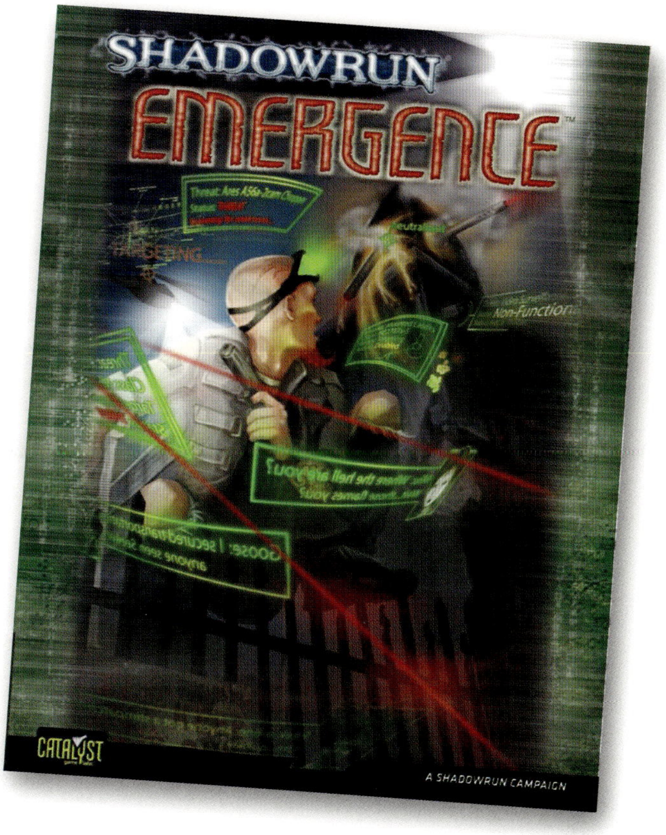

The book was about the emergence of persons who had the ability to communicate with and control computers with their minds alone. It was introducing a completely new concept from previous editions and was to be used as a new historical reference guide for the universe.

The direction wasn't so simple. There was to be a man escaping a militarized prison. He had to be wearing a straight-jacket, with violent chaos going on all around him as distractions for his escape. There were to be turret-mounted machine guns shooting at him from above. Security vehicles and flying drones were misbehaving, engaging each other, and/or simply self-destructing. Security alarms were going off, other prisoners were trying to escape, guns were blazing, all of this at night.... and HE was to be shown as the one responsible for it all. It had to be clear in the illustration that he did not have a single circuit of cybernetic enhancement. There should also be hovering augmented reality windows around his head to illustrate his abilities even further. In order to deliberately impress that this person had no cybernetic assistance - it was suggested (later made mandatory) that he should be bald and that I show the back 3/4 of his head (this is where the old versions of cybernetic head implants would usually be installed).

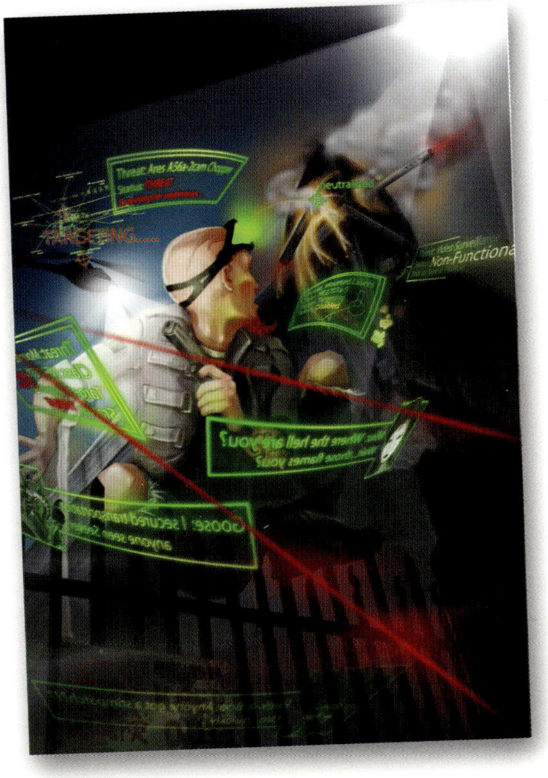

The most challenging part was to show the close-up of the head from behind (to show the lack of cybernetics) as well as show the aerial forces assaulting him - including the mandatory rooftop machine guns and flying vehicles.

I warped the augmented reality windows around him to allude that they were somehow different than the normal ones in other illustrations. Tough assignment - but it led to more.

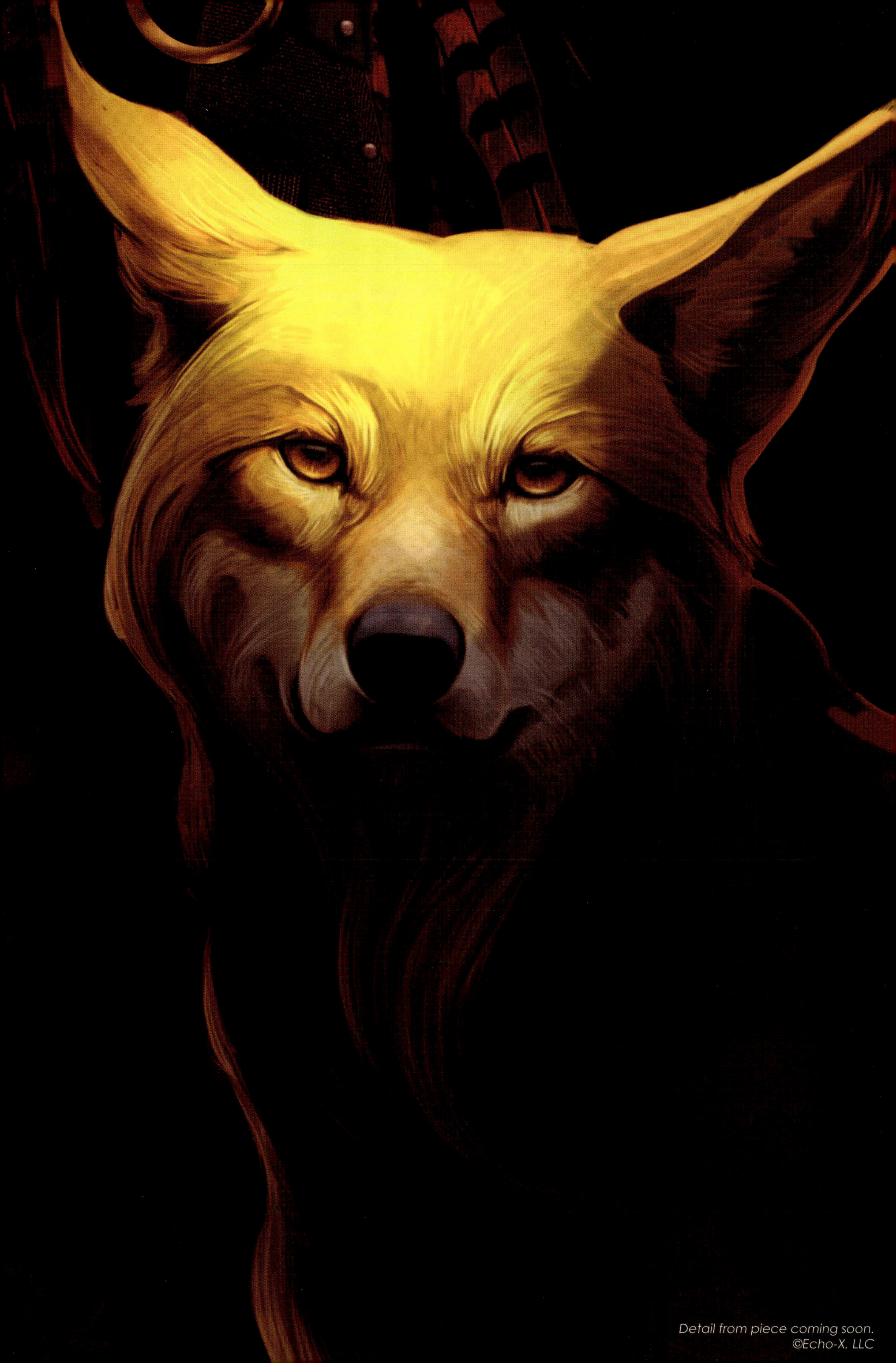

Detail from piece coming soon.

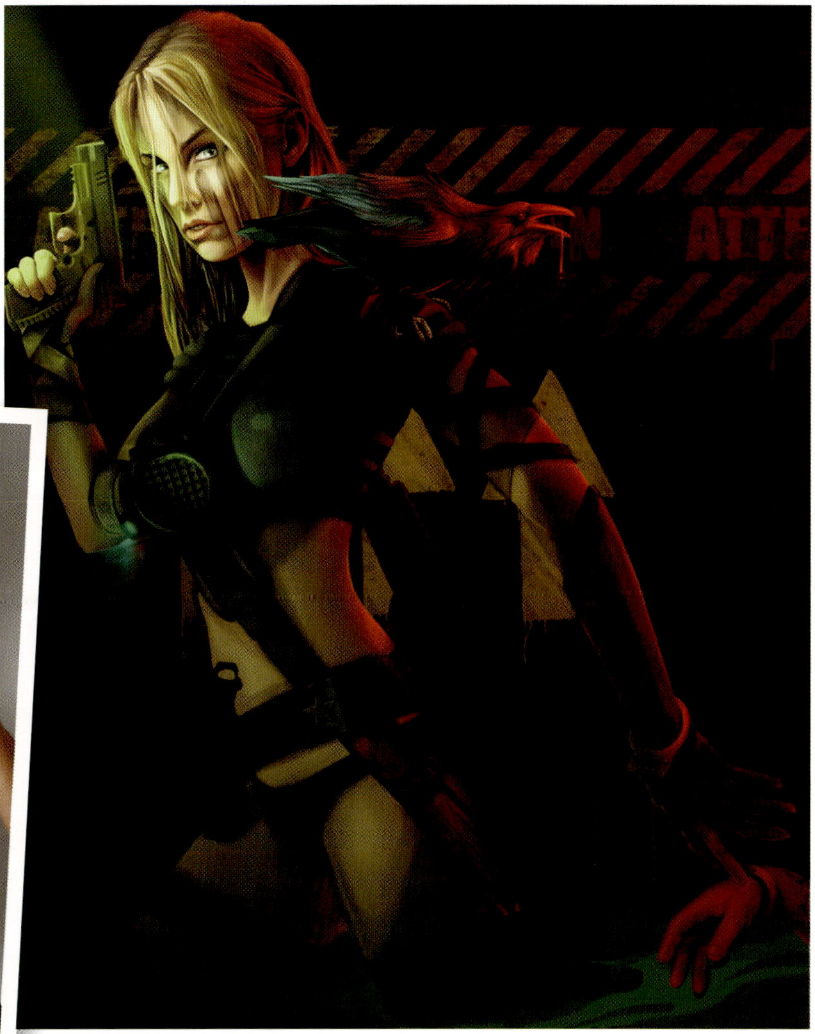

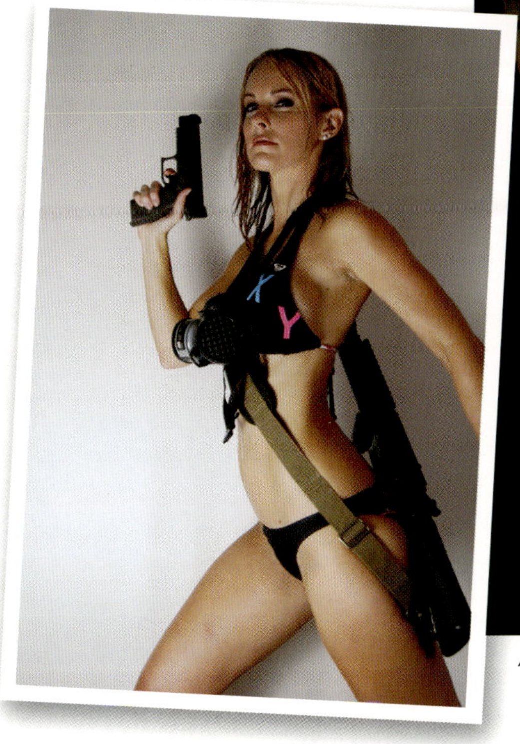

Angela rocked this shoot. ©Echo-X, LLC

Character Design

Characters may sometimes be imagined by a writer – but the artist is the one who infuses them with life and imprints them into the reader's memory. It is critical for an Artist to intimately understand the character before the first drawing is made. I enjoy most when I am given the freedom to develop and illustrate my own character designs. I take this very seriously, not just because it's my job, but because I am really and truly passionate about the genre. Creating and breathing life into characters is what I specialize in, and it is what people love most about my work.

Even a supposedly minor character, such as a red wolf (left), will get my full attention. She's not merely a prop in the scene, but has a life of her own – proud, alert, and indignant to your presence.

Whenever I can, I make sure to introduce story elements that will tease the viewer and suggest the greater picture of that character's life. Sometimes it is simply the gesture of the character or perhaps the lighting, but often it is the small details in the eyes, the clothing, the scars, and the affectations, that are chosen with love and purpose that bring them to life.

In one piece, a wet woman is sloshing through some darkly lit subterranean tunnel filled waist-deep with water, light illuminating her face from above. An angry raven, blood pouring from it's mouth, is staring at something unseen in her wake. He is viciously lit by a red bulb behind them symbolizing some very recent violence. Only last are you drawn to left wrist, which bears a handcuff dragging a limp body through the scene. What could possibly be going on here? I leave that up to the viewer to decide.

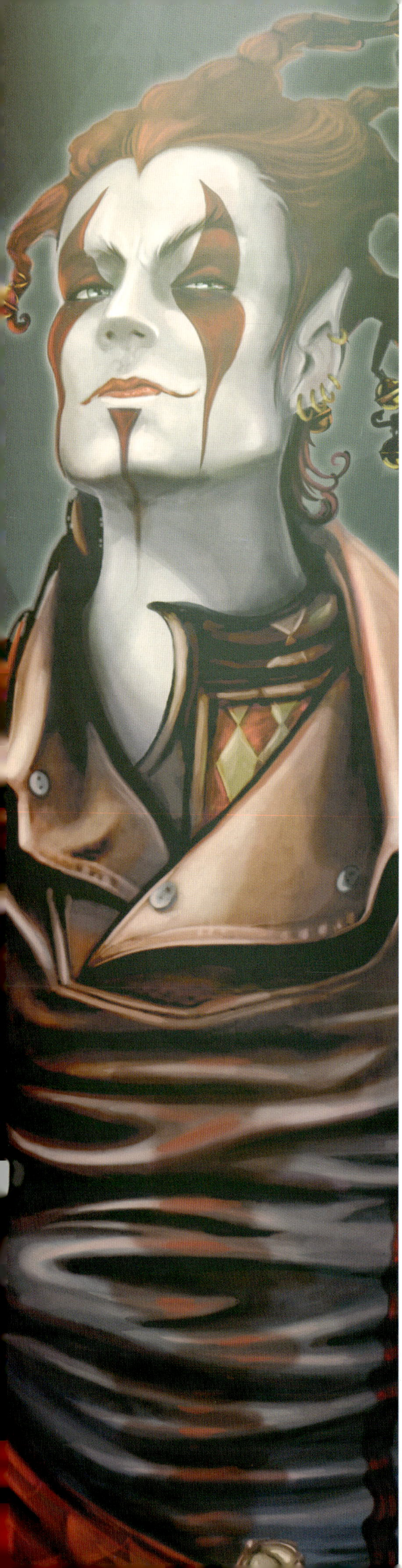

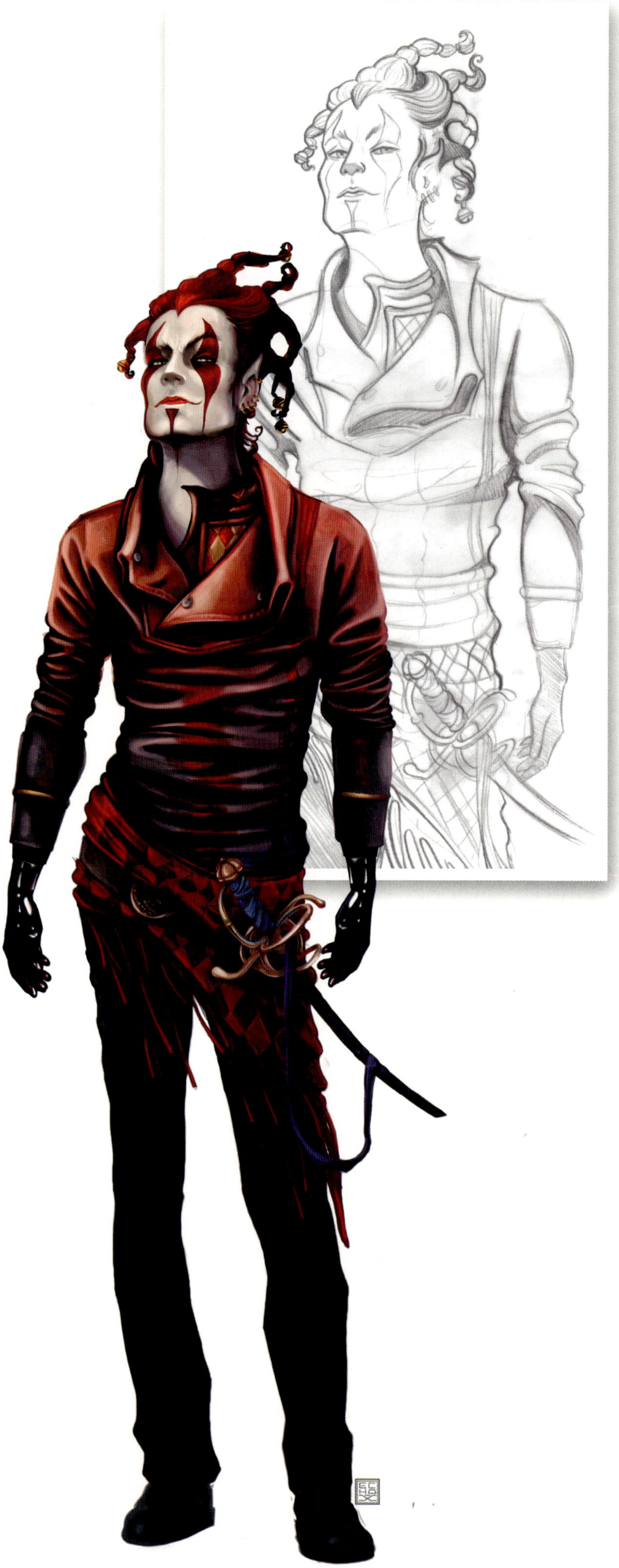

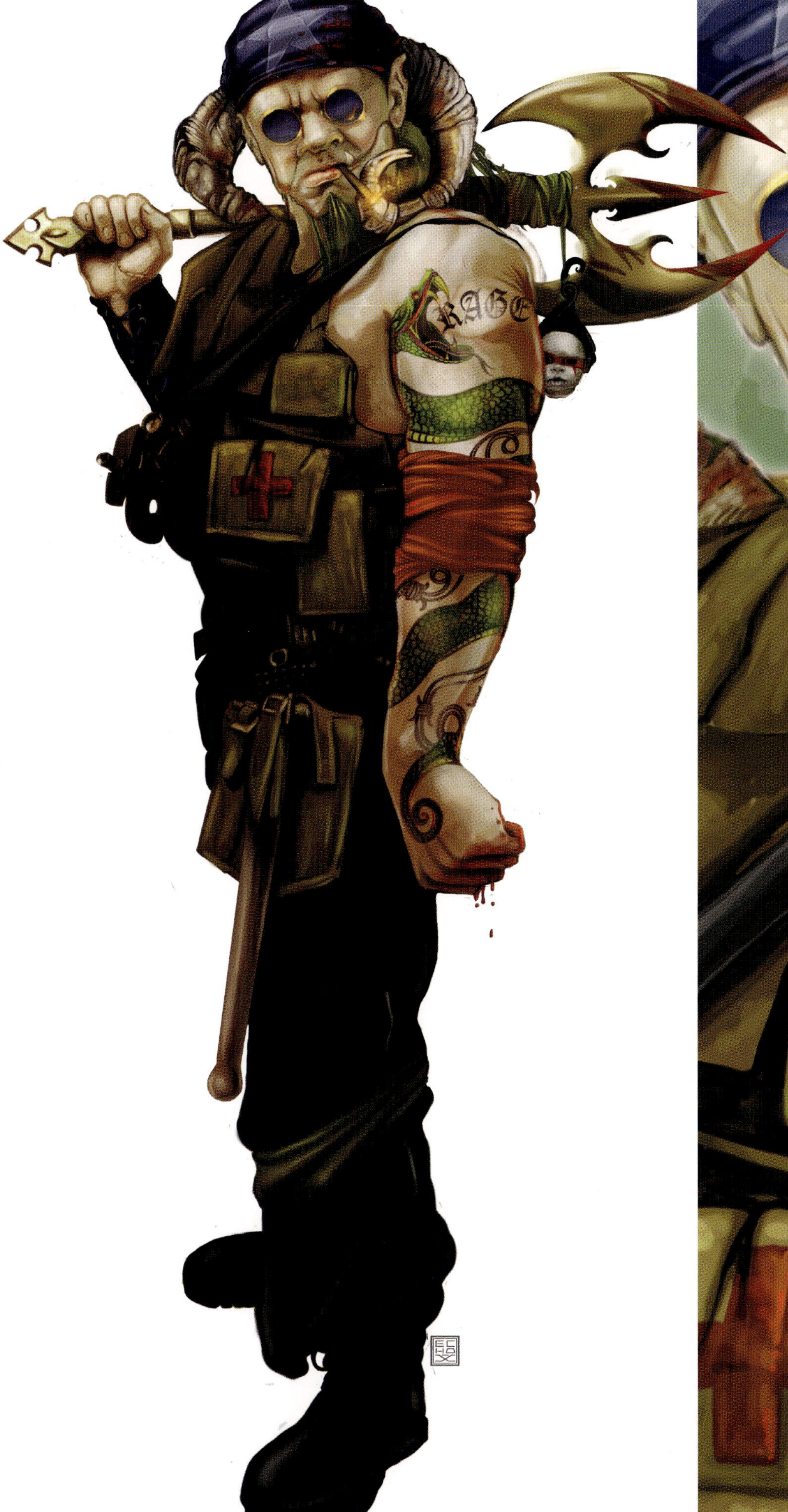
RAGE
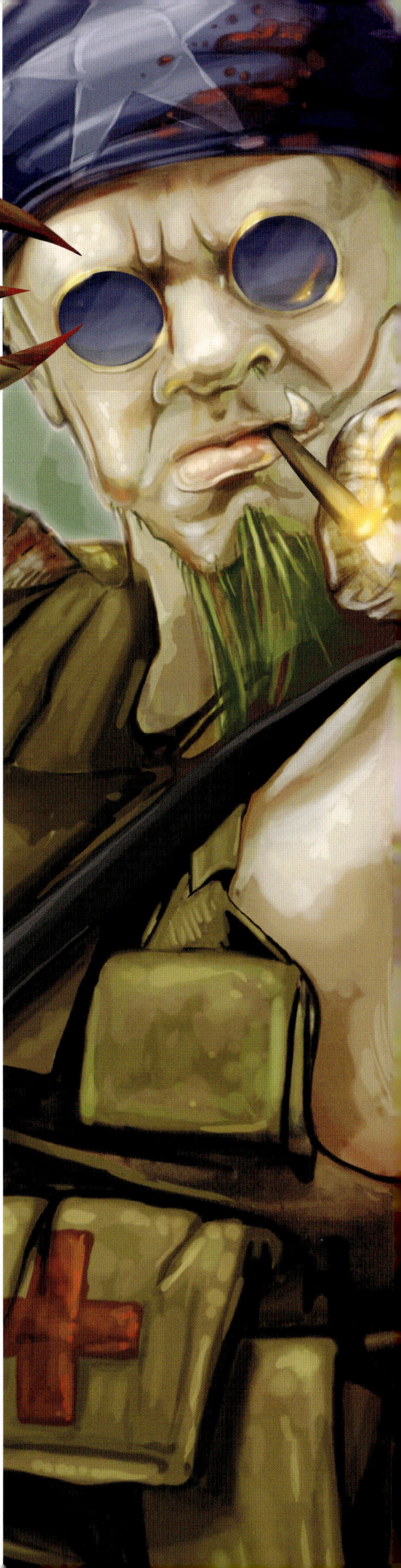

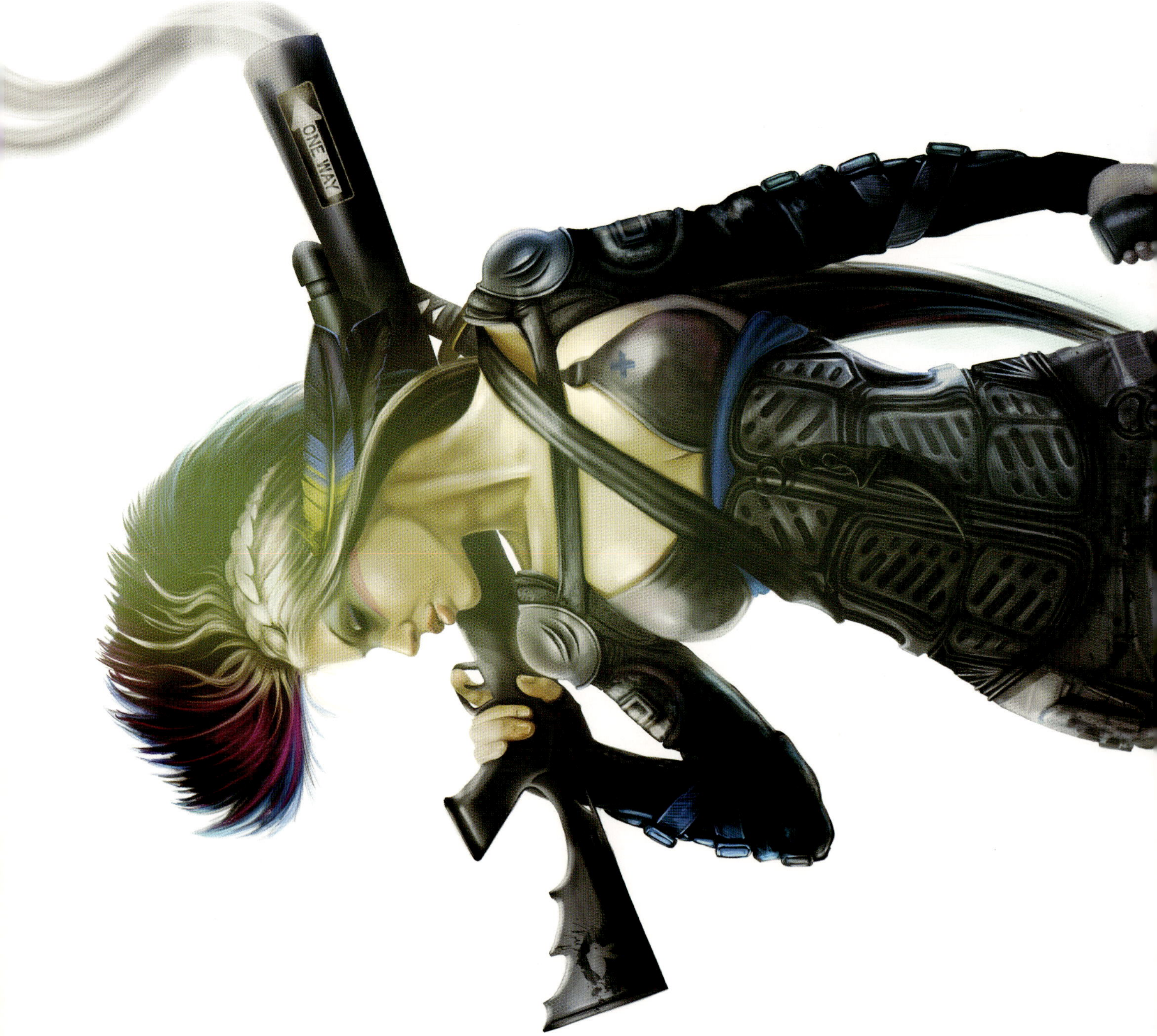
ONE WAY

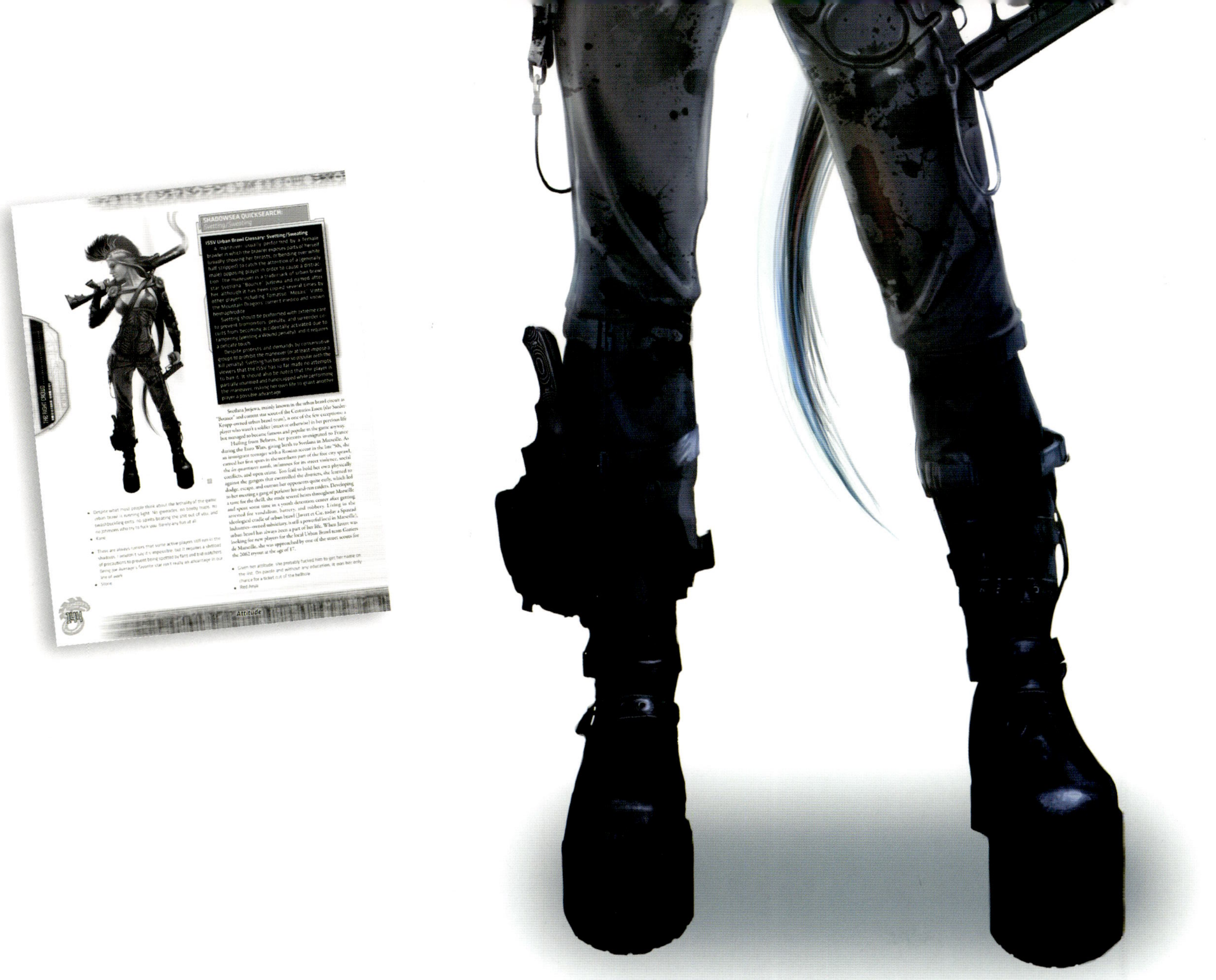

Svetlana Jurjewa ©InMediaRes, LLC

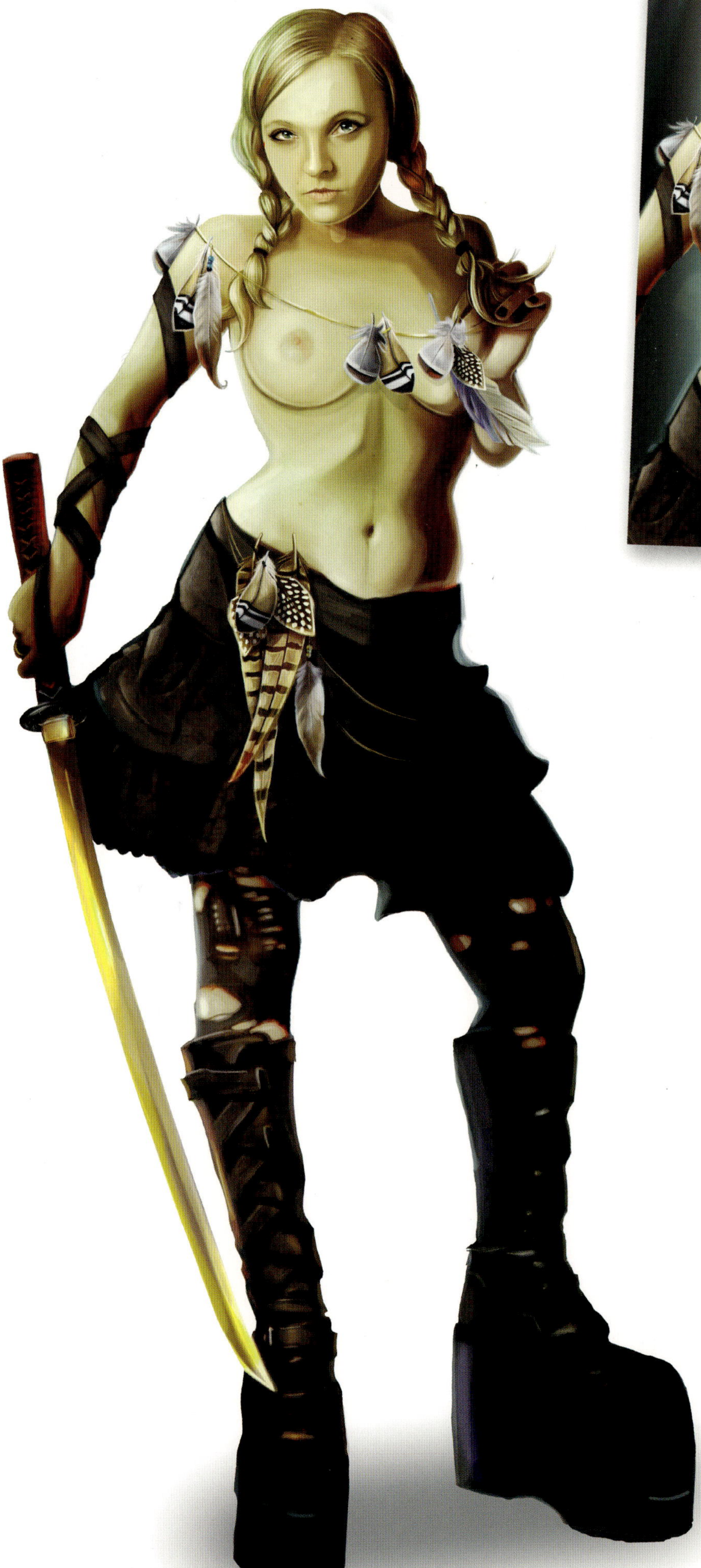

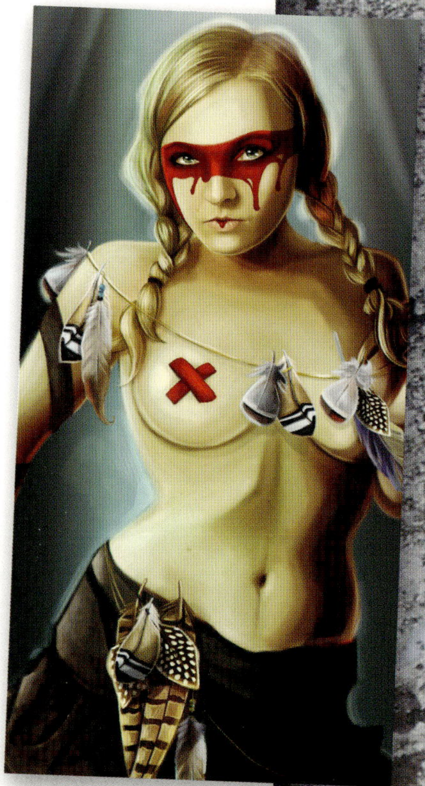

Tape ©Echo-X, LLC

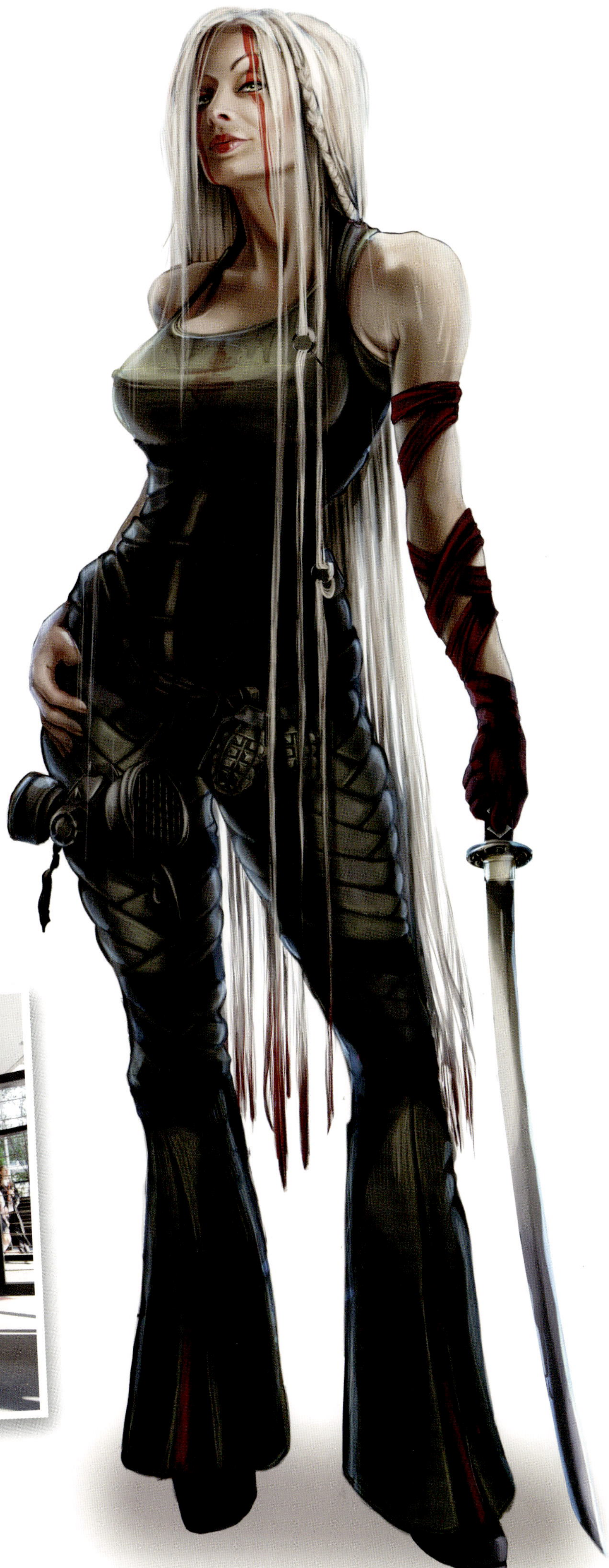

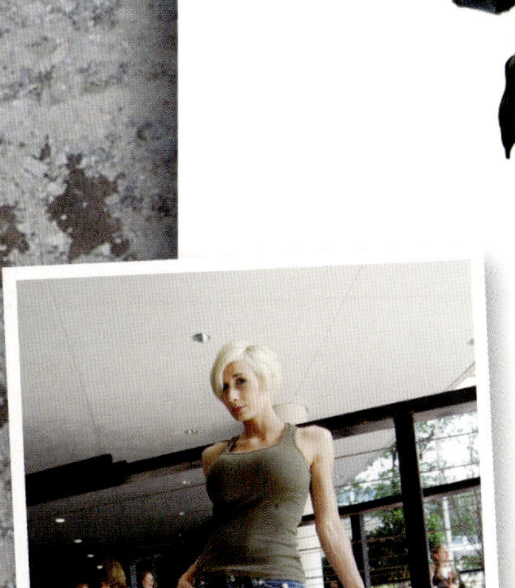

Whette ©Echo-X, LLC

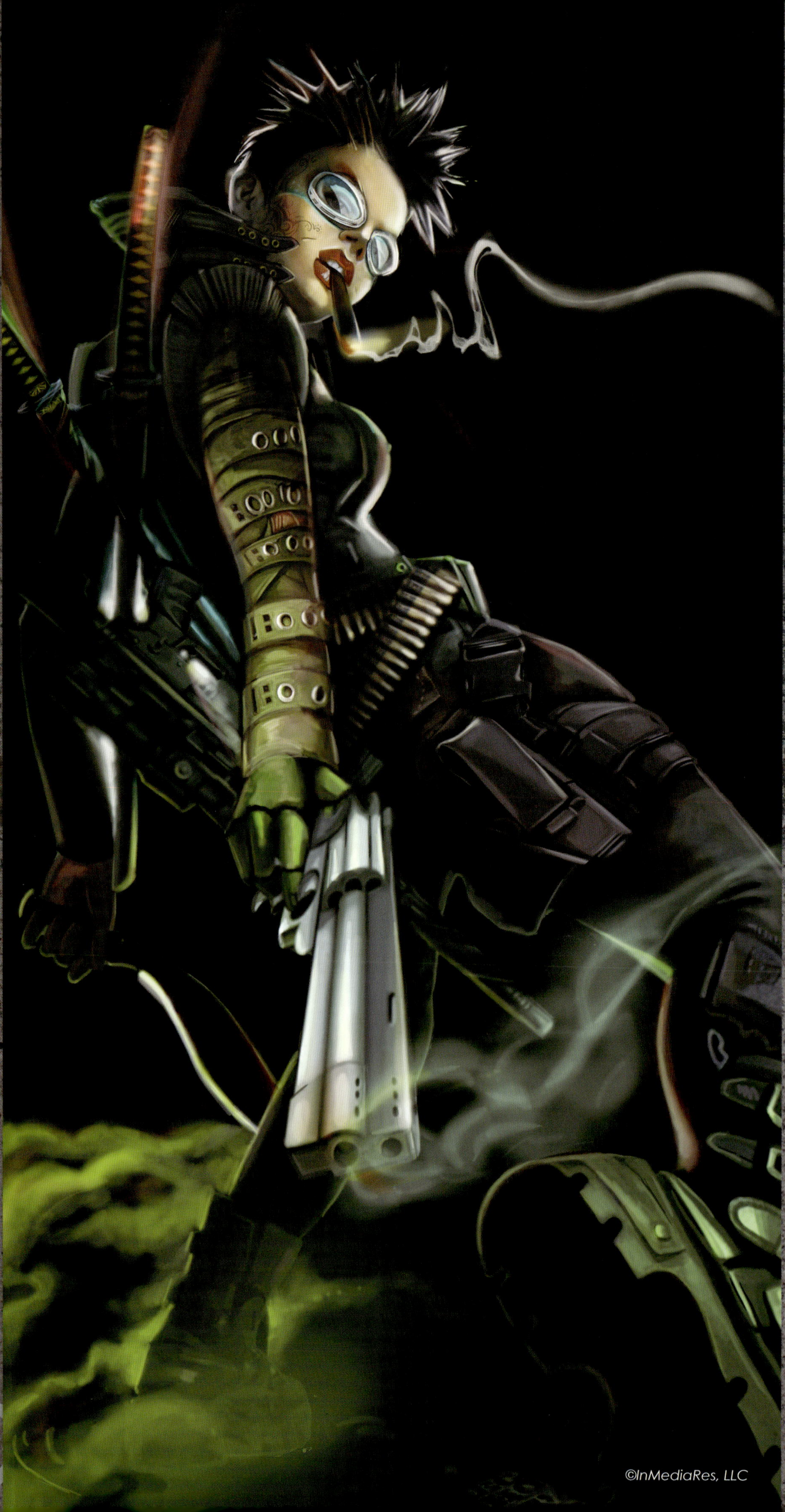

©InMediaRes, LLC

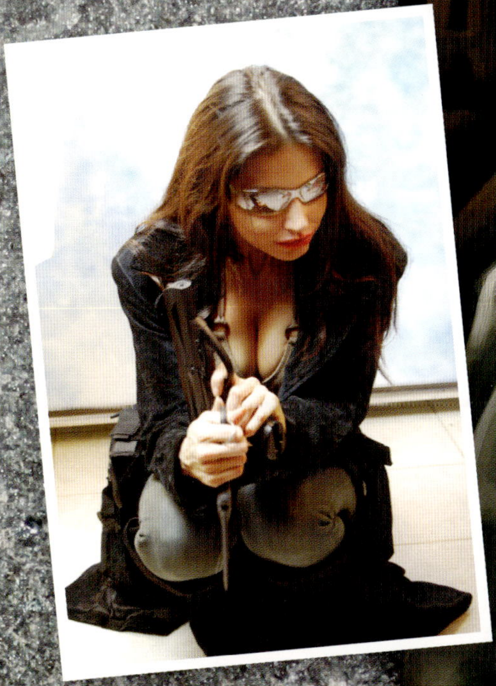

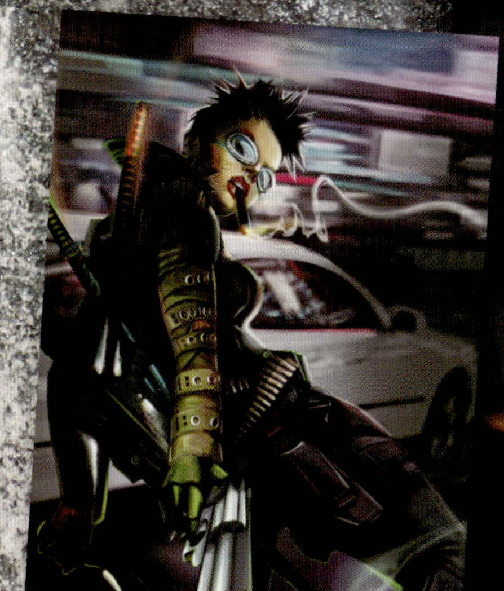

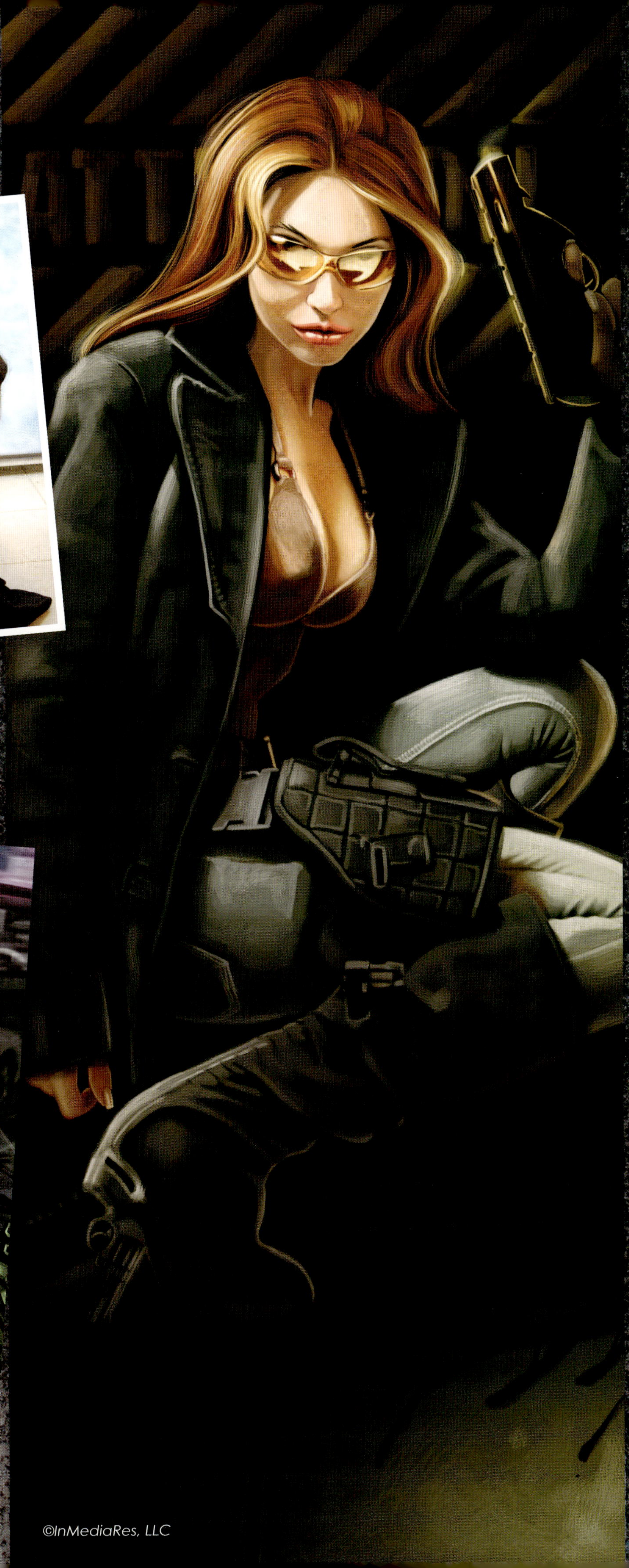

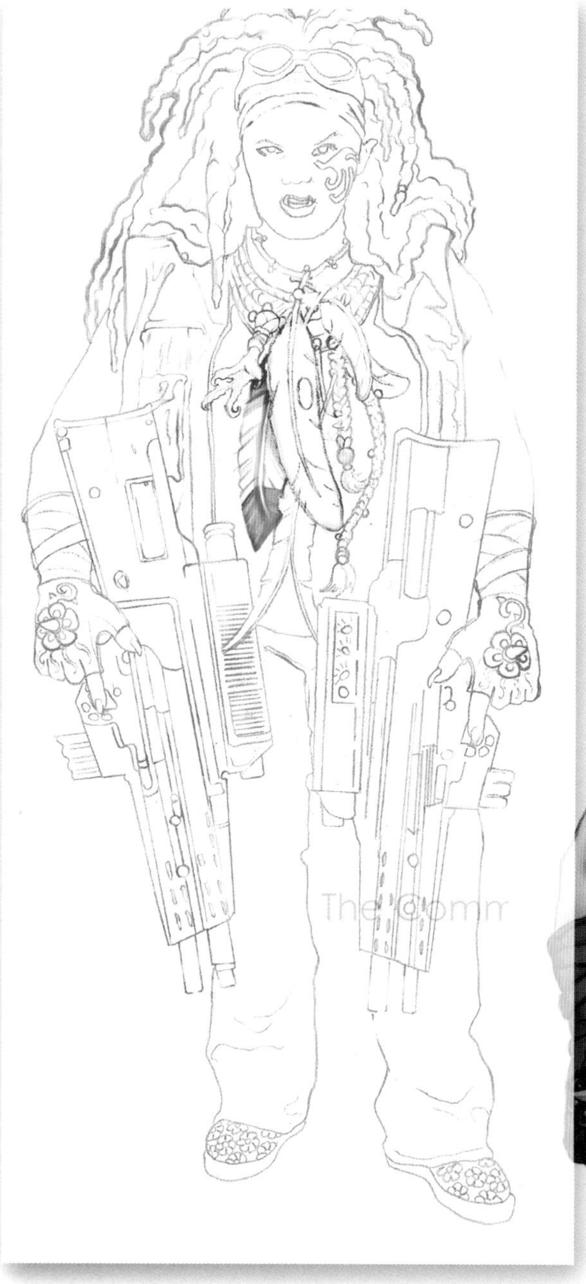

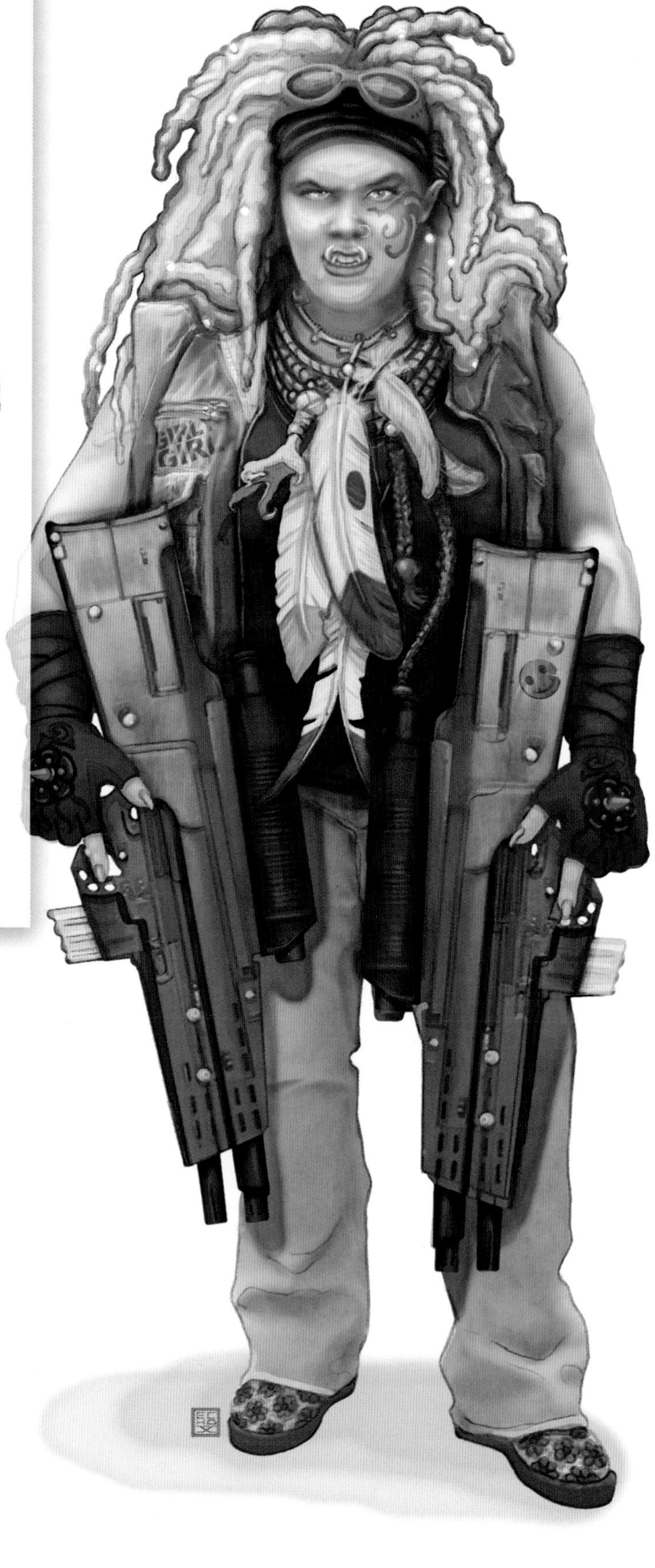

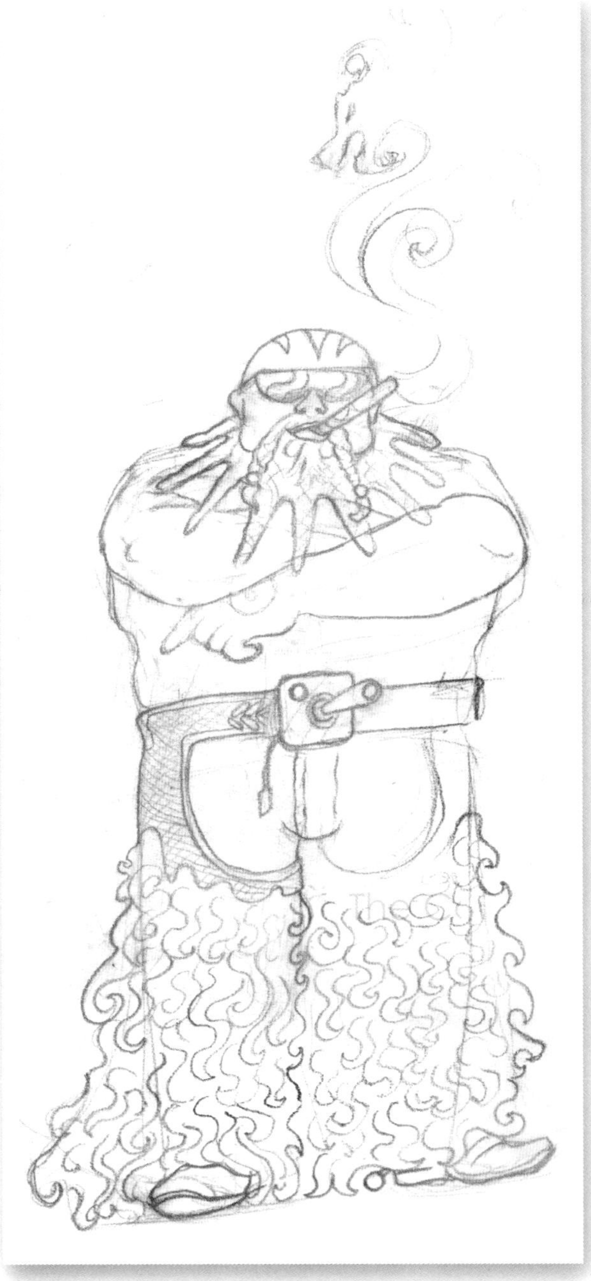

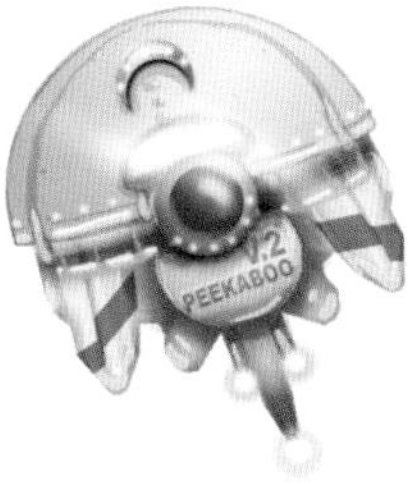
V2
PEEKABOO

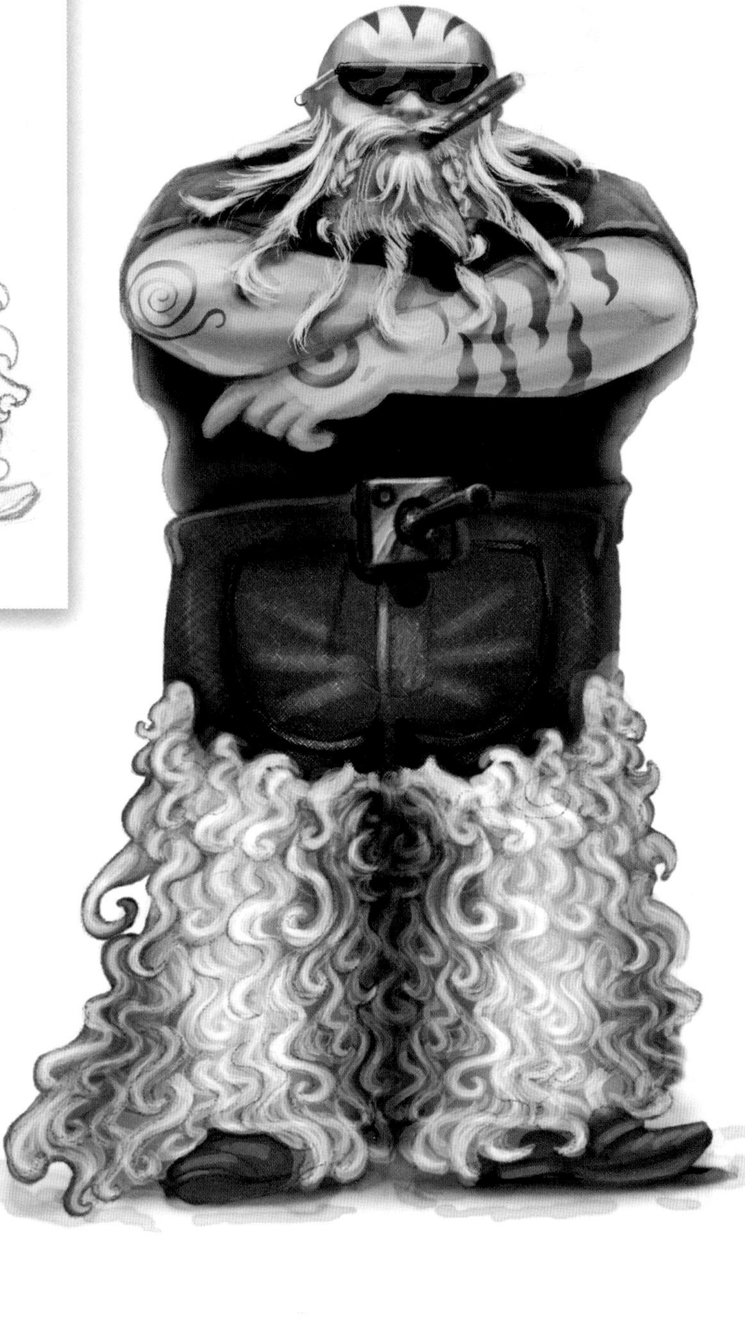

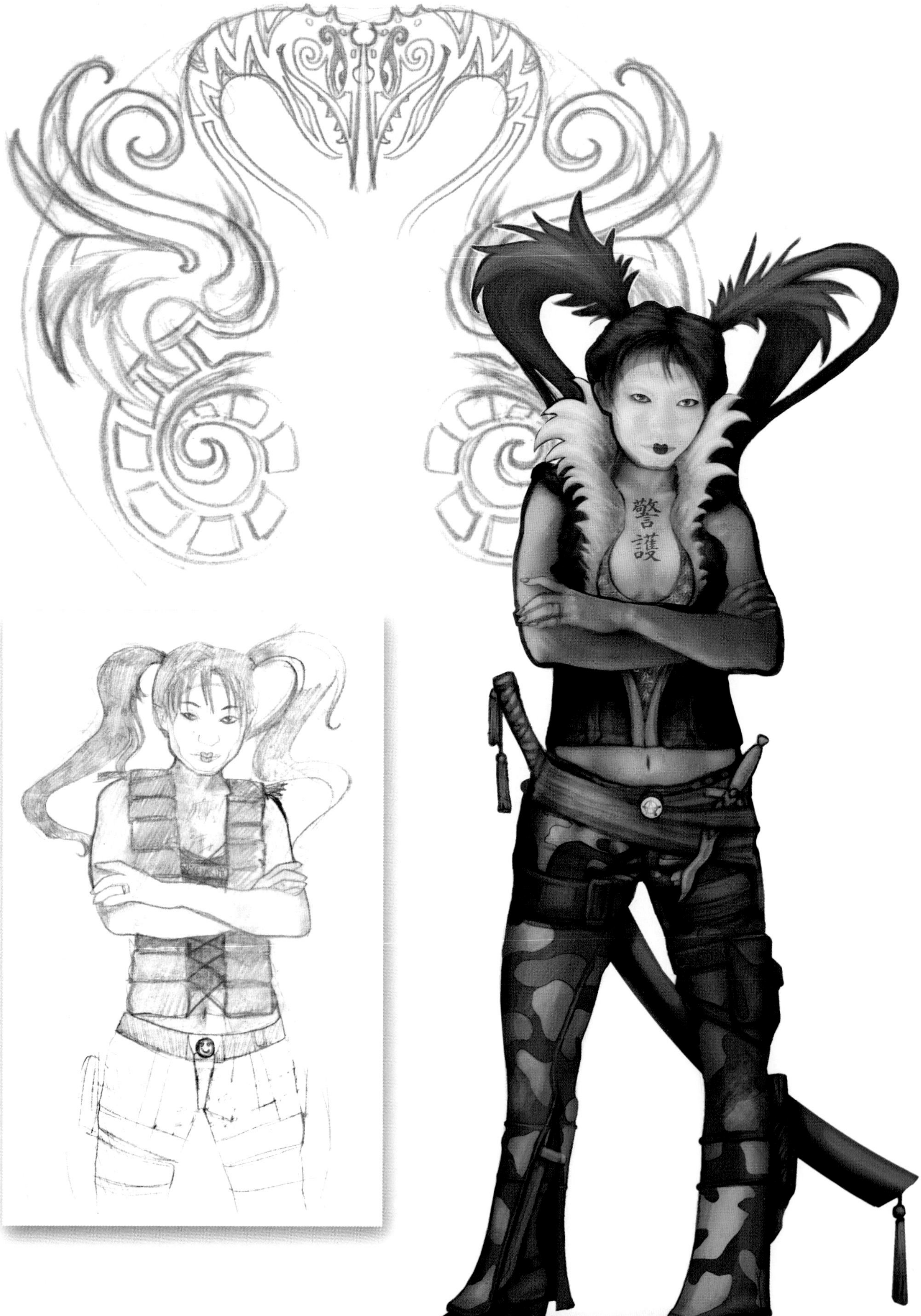

Human ©2005 InMediaRes, LLC

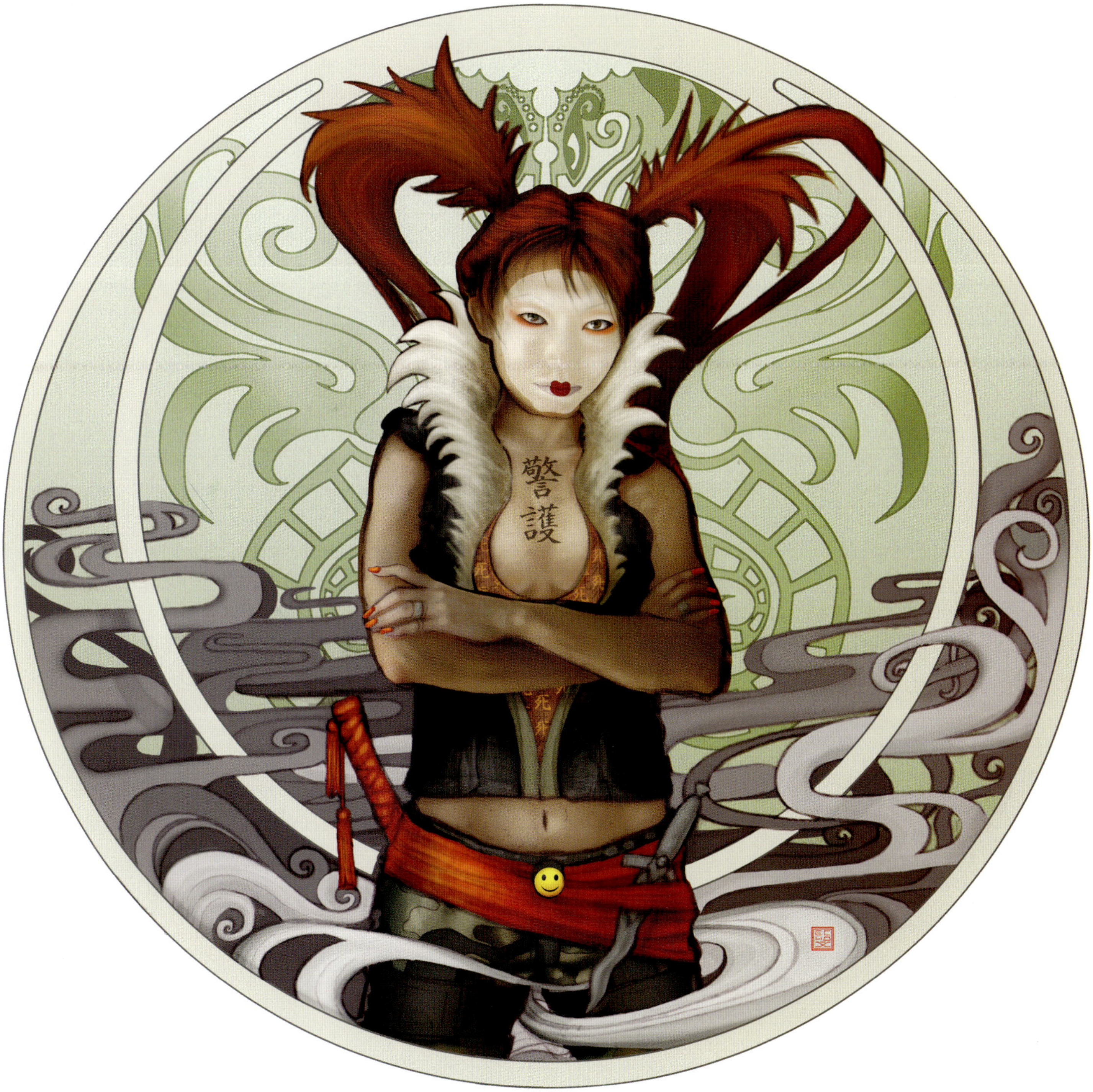

I did this piece for myself two years before Catalyst hired me. I liked her so much, I just added legs, removed the background, and removed the colors.

Escort ©Echo-X, LLC

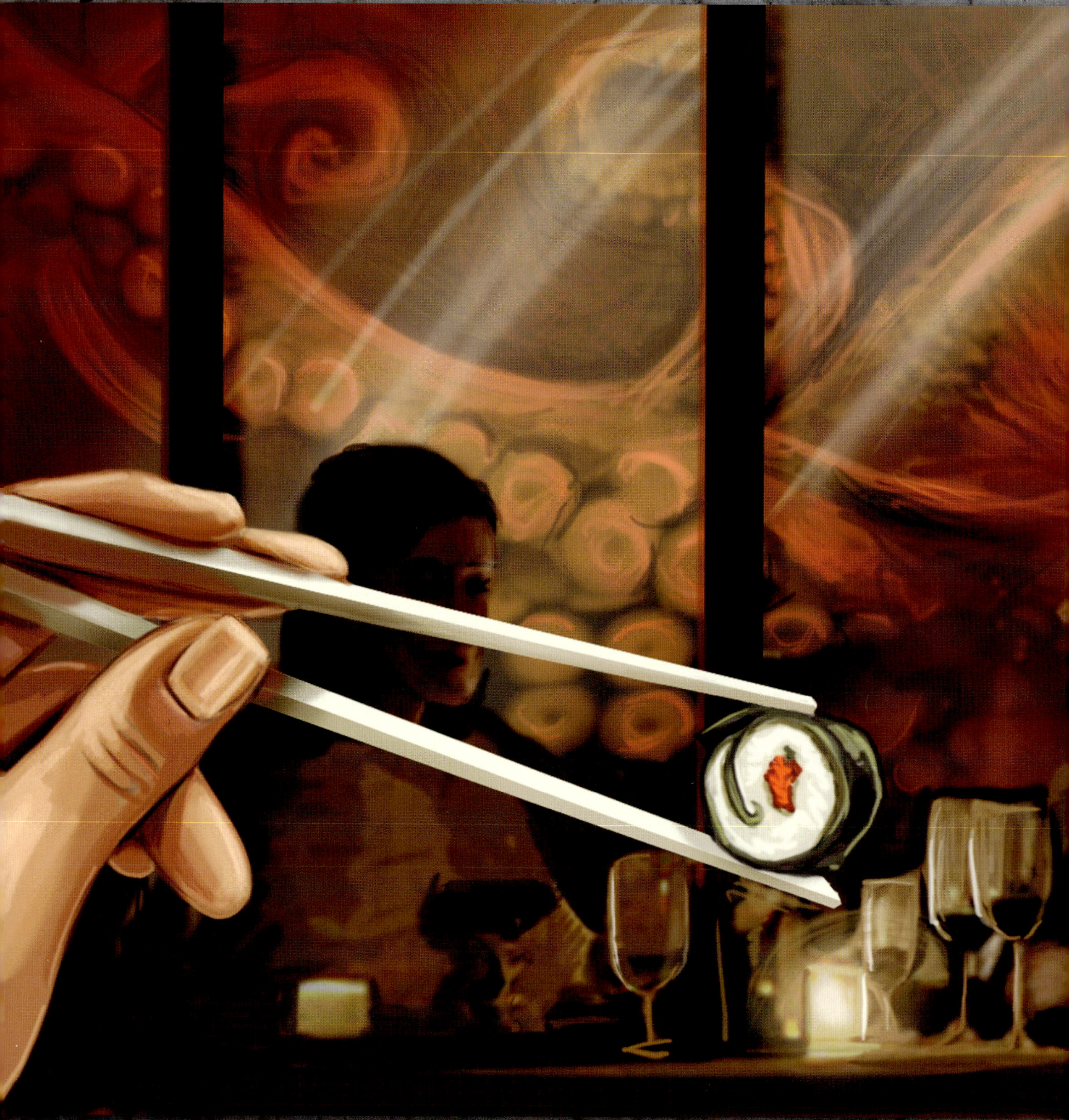

This is a simple scene for a restaurant location in the game. My art direction was to create and illustrate the upscale environment of the establishment. My favorite part of this scene is the intimacy of the date. Notice that it's a woman's hand feeding sushi to her date on the right.

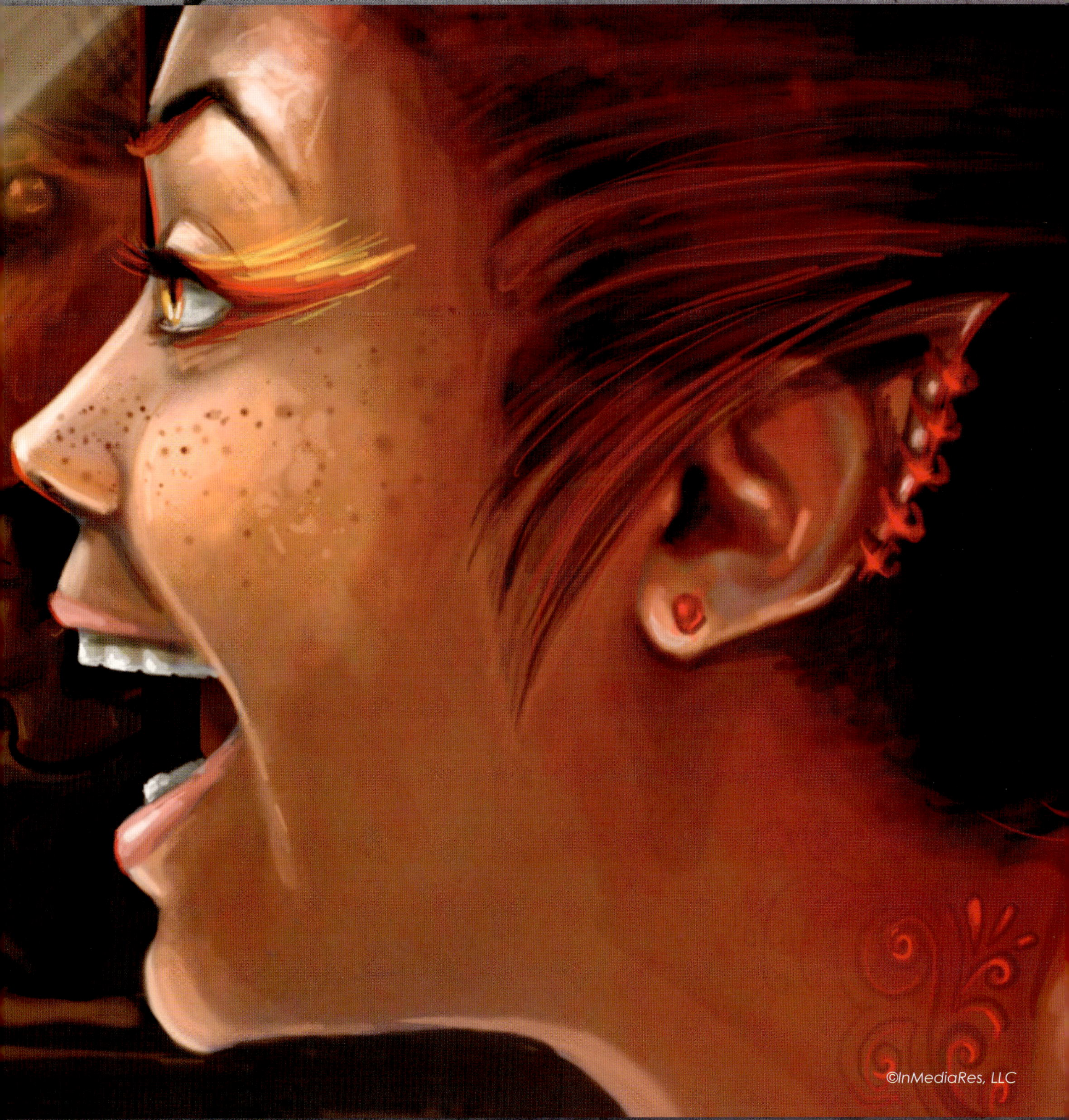
©InMediaRes, LLC

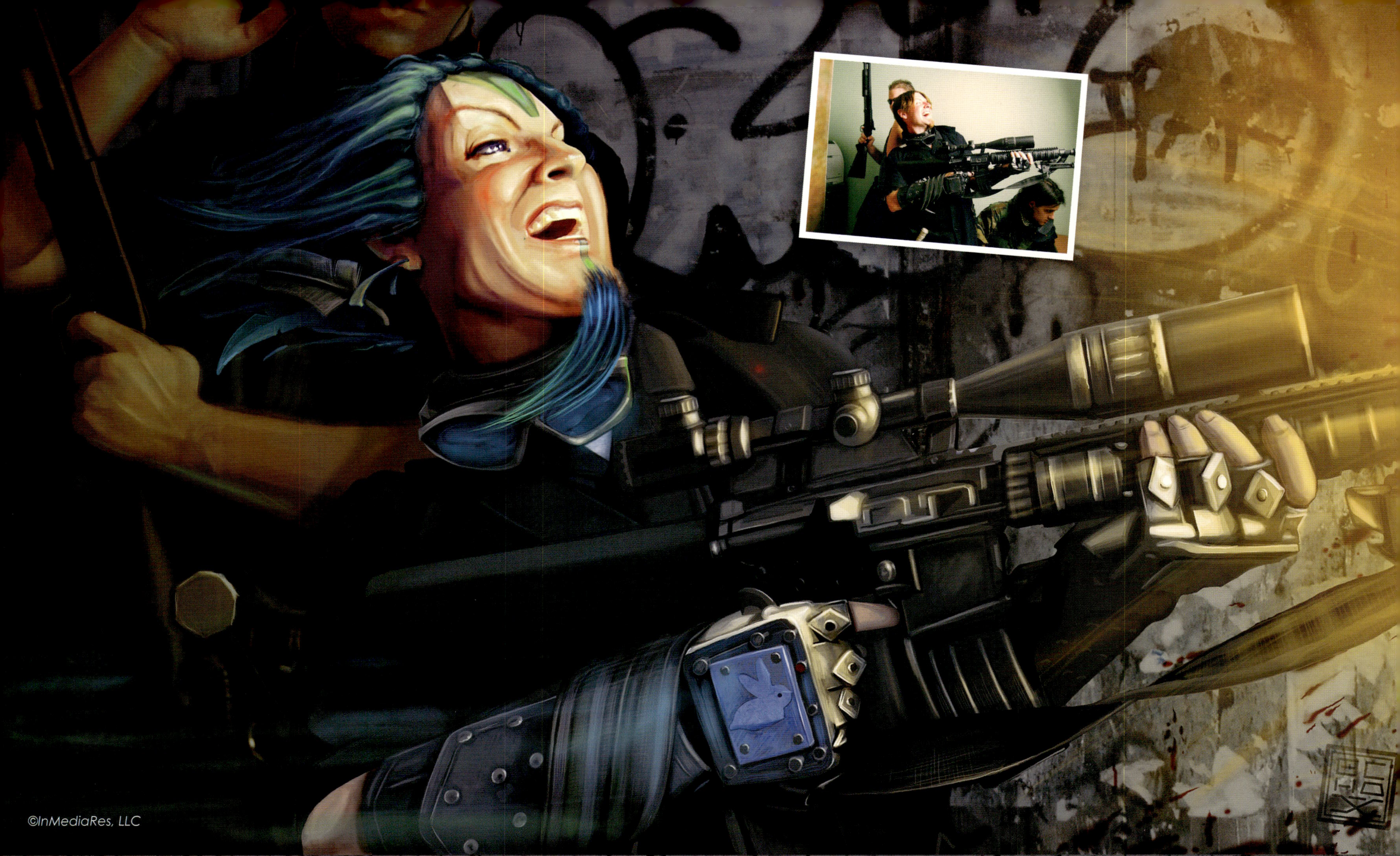

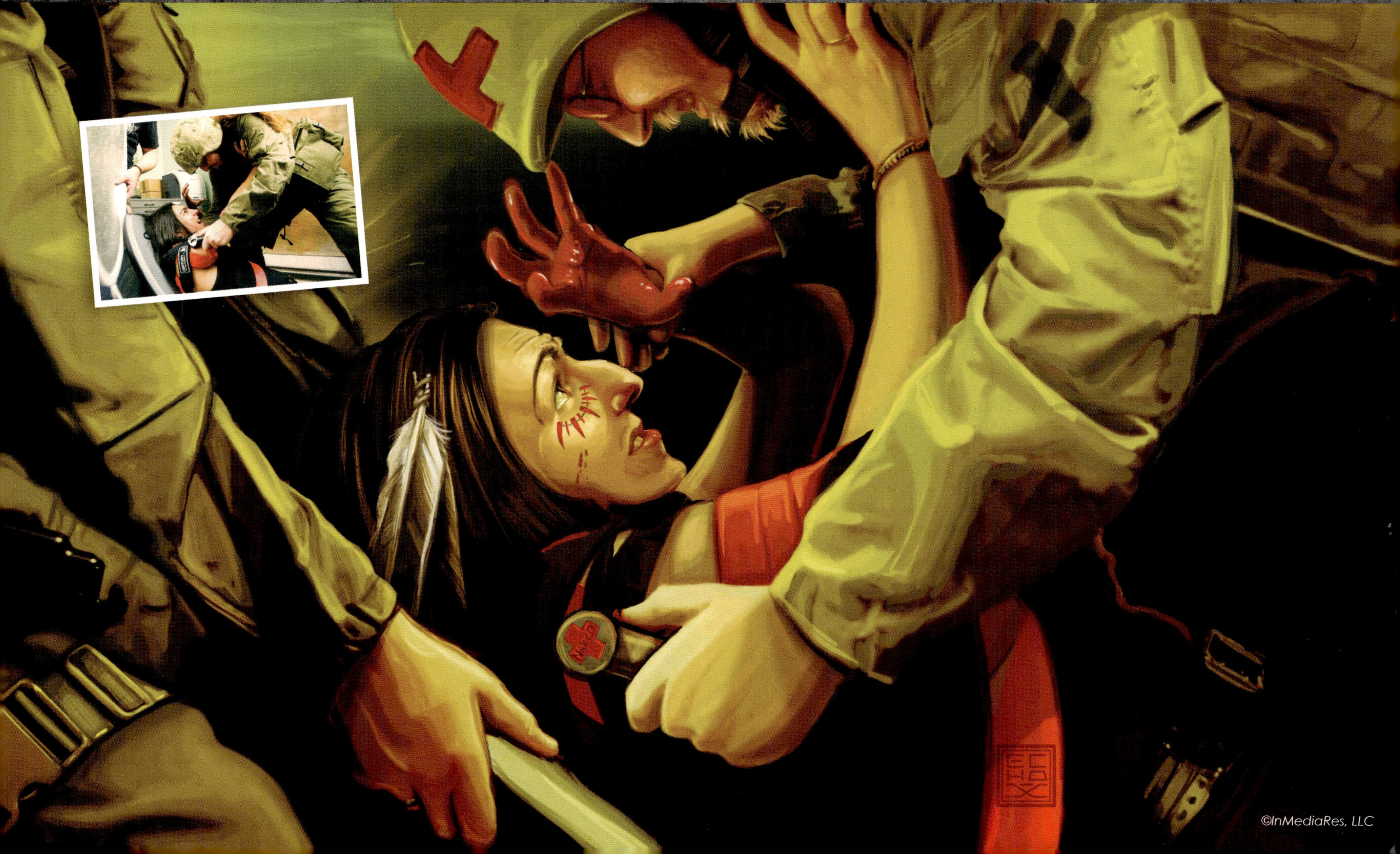

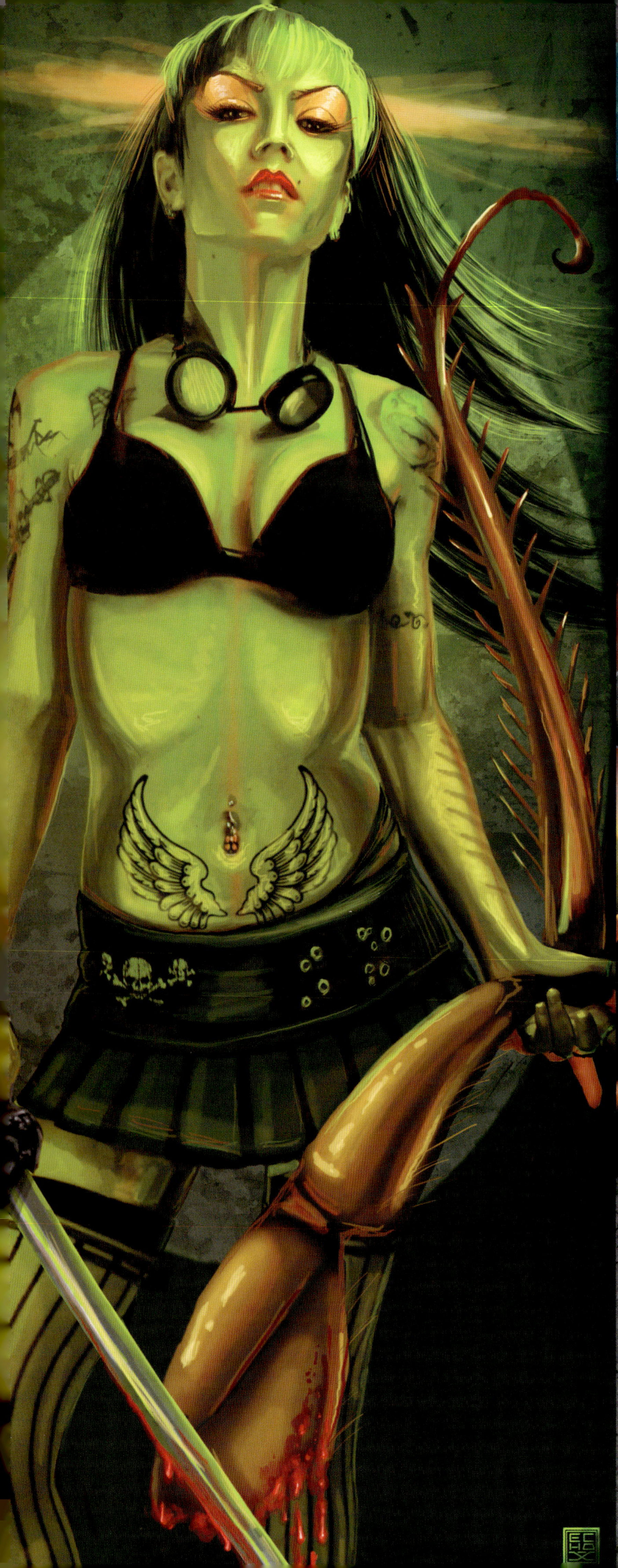

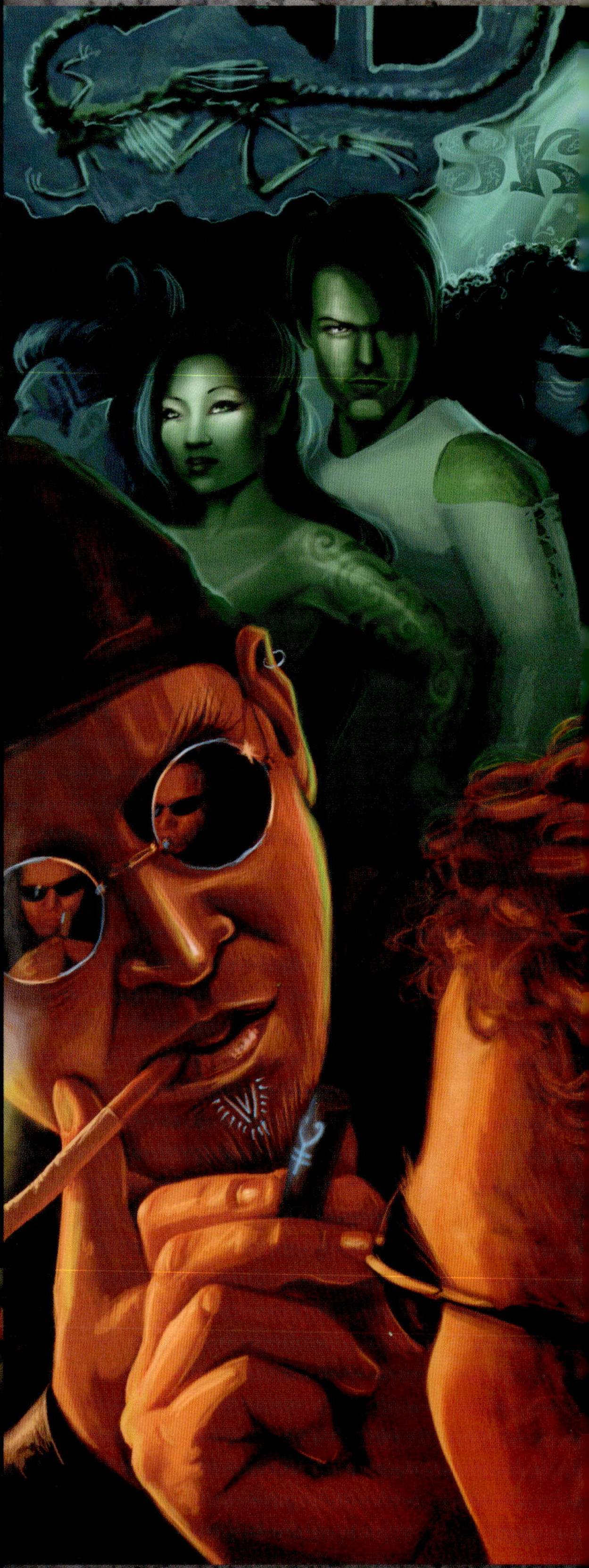

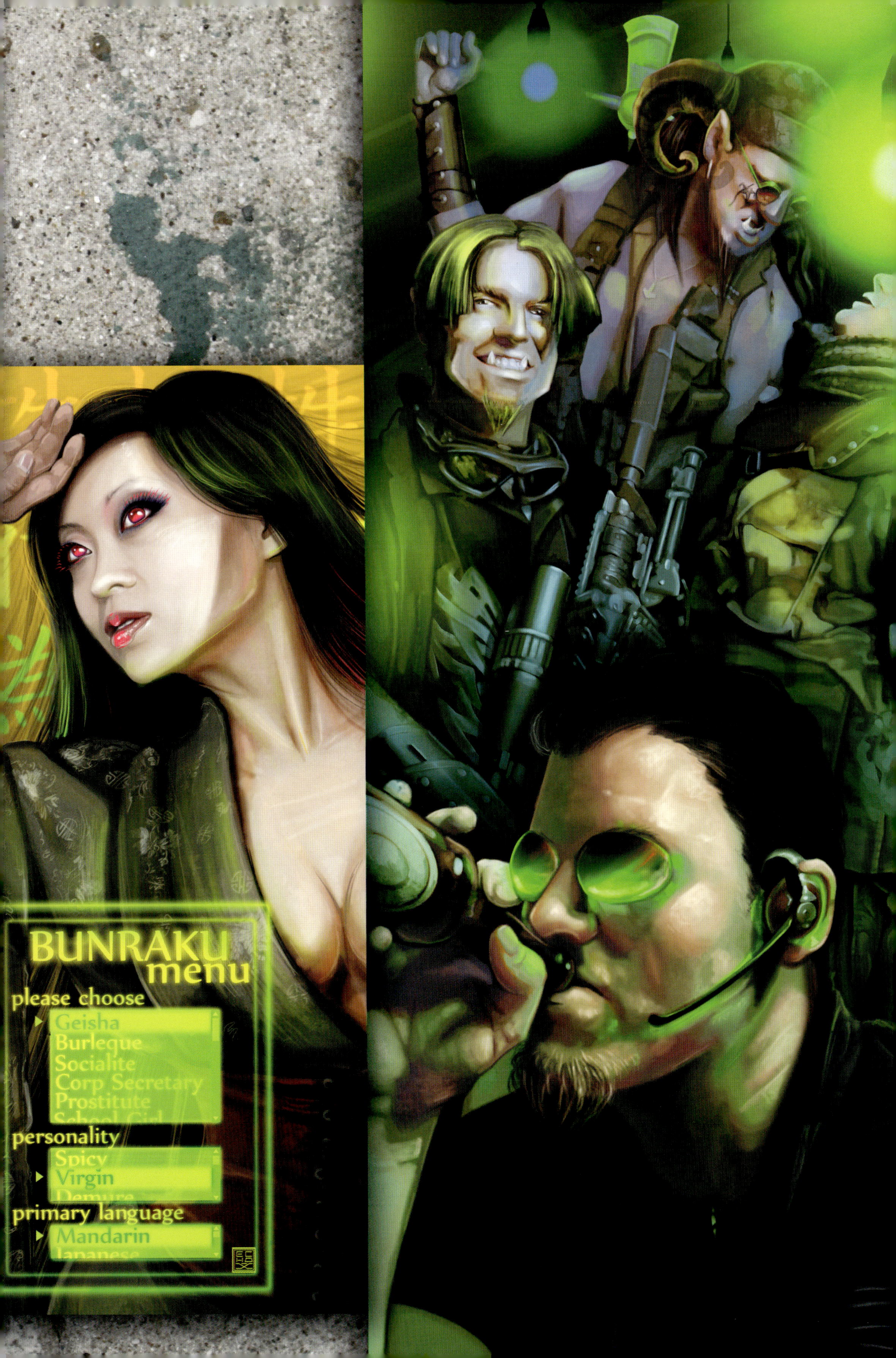
BUNRAKU
menu
please choose
Geisha
Burleque
Socialite
Corp Secretary
Prostitute
personality
Spicy
Virgin
primary language
Mandarin

Brooklyn

I envision that my career looks rather like a successful Shadowrunner's lair. On the street level is a marvelously successful loft featuring a pristine display case of a lifetimes worth of karma, sweat, and tears. My portfolio is proudly filled with the highest quality work, the largest name brand clients and numerous awards around the world. However just to the right of the awards – and carefully set in shadow – there is a door that leads under the stairs.

Behind that door is my personal space and sanctum sactorum. My lodge* is a playground of inspiration where props such as gas masks, tentacles, and karambits hang near my workstation. It is a place that Madison Avenue may not quite understand. Here, those who understand great passion will appreciate my influences as much as my poster designs. I will never give up my love of mainstream work, but just as equally, I will never give up my geek.

It was 1993-1999 in Brooklyn, New York. I was a Junior at Pratt Institute, I met Lazarus Chernik. On our second date, he introduced me to Shadowrun and I was immediately hooked. (Yes, I married the GM.)

The following years were "a major contributing factor" to my artistic style. I can think of nothing more Shadowrunny than eeking an existence solely as a freelancer in the New York sprawl. We were creative temps within the megacorps of Manhattan on Park Avenue, Times Square, Rockefeller Center, the World Financial Center, and the Twin Towers. Lazarus and I gamed while we rode the subway in the wee hours of the night, and subsisted on $0.99 cent packs of hot dogs when we had barely a cent to our name. We walked the city often. Sometimes we didn't have the $1.25 to ride the subway, but usually because of the sights. I was amazed at the homeless villages that erupted under the highways, the gangs, the prostitutes, and the media glitz. We revelled in meeting people of all ethnicities, sexual appetites, the rich, the wage slaves, the gangrenous homeless, and believers of every religion and none. Together. On the subway and in the glittering city there were characters. There were so many characters. I was illustrating. We were in love.

There and then, I found myself. Characters, details, ornaments, attitudes, affectations, stories, symbols, foreshadowing, illusions and allusions, diversity - working their way into every thread of my body of work. I hope you enjoy it.

* *A Shadowrun term.*

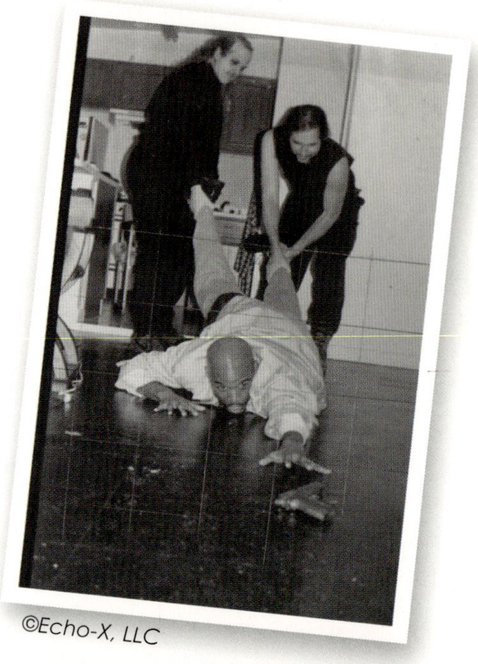

©Echo-X, LLC

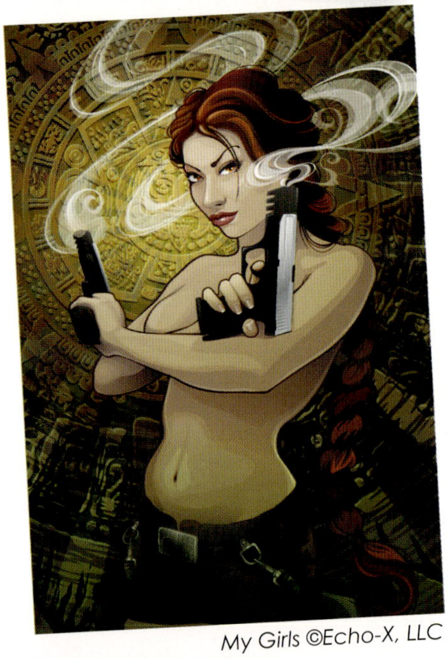

My Girls ©Echo-X, LLC

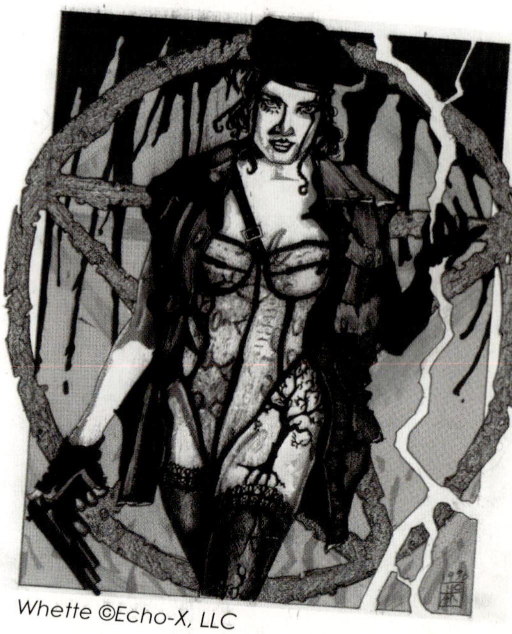

Whette ©Echo-X, LLC

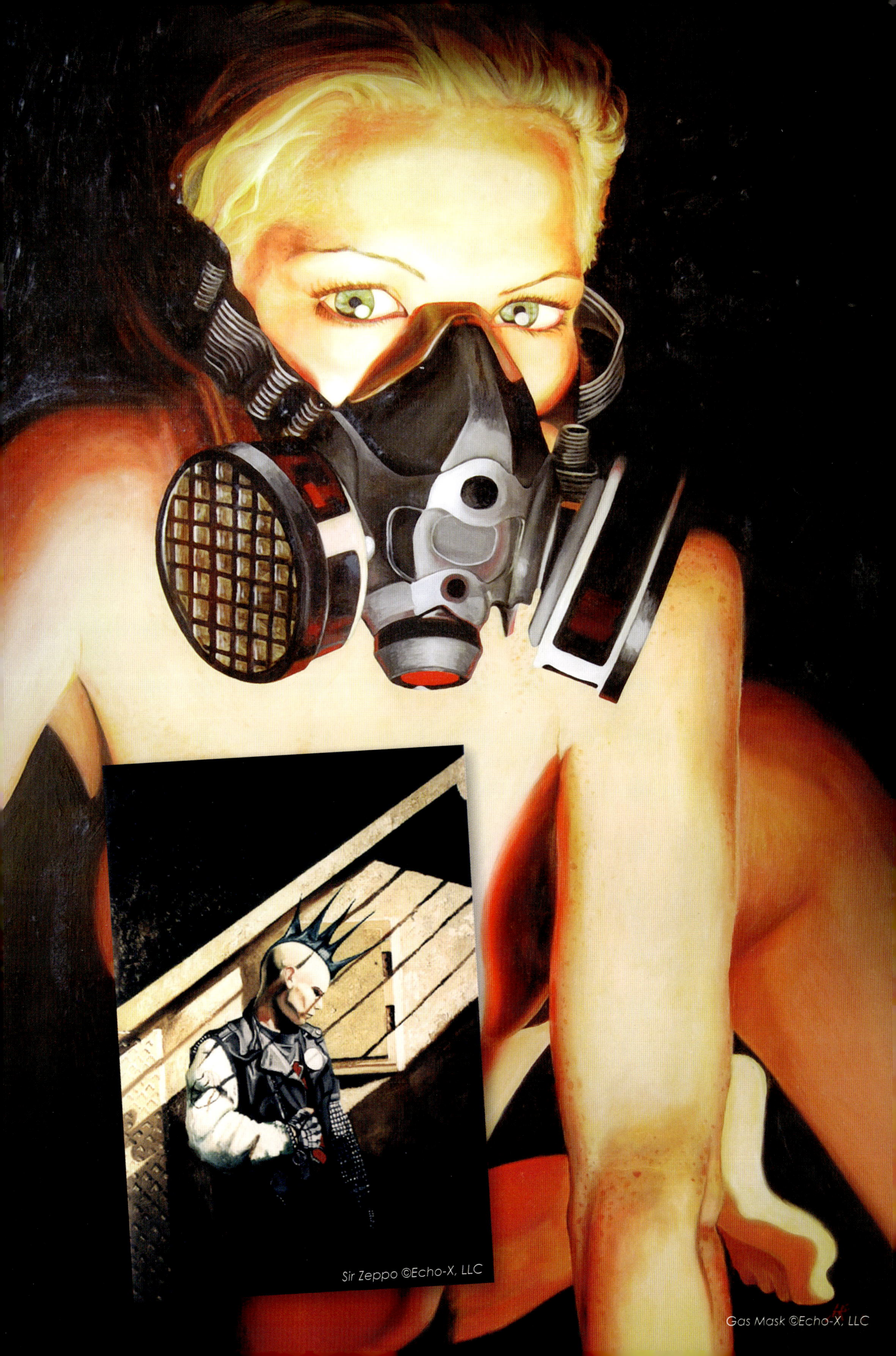

Gas Mask ©Echo-X, LLC

Sir Zeppo ©Echo-X, LLC

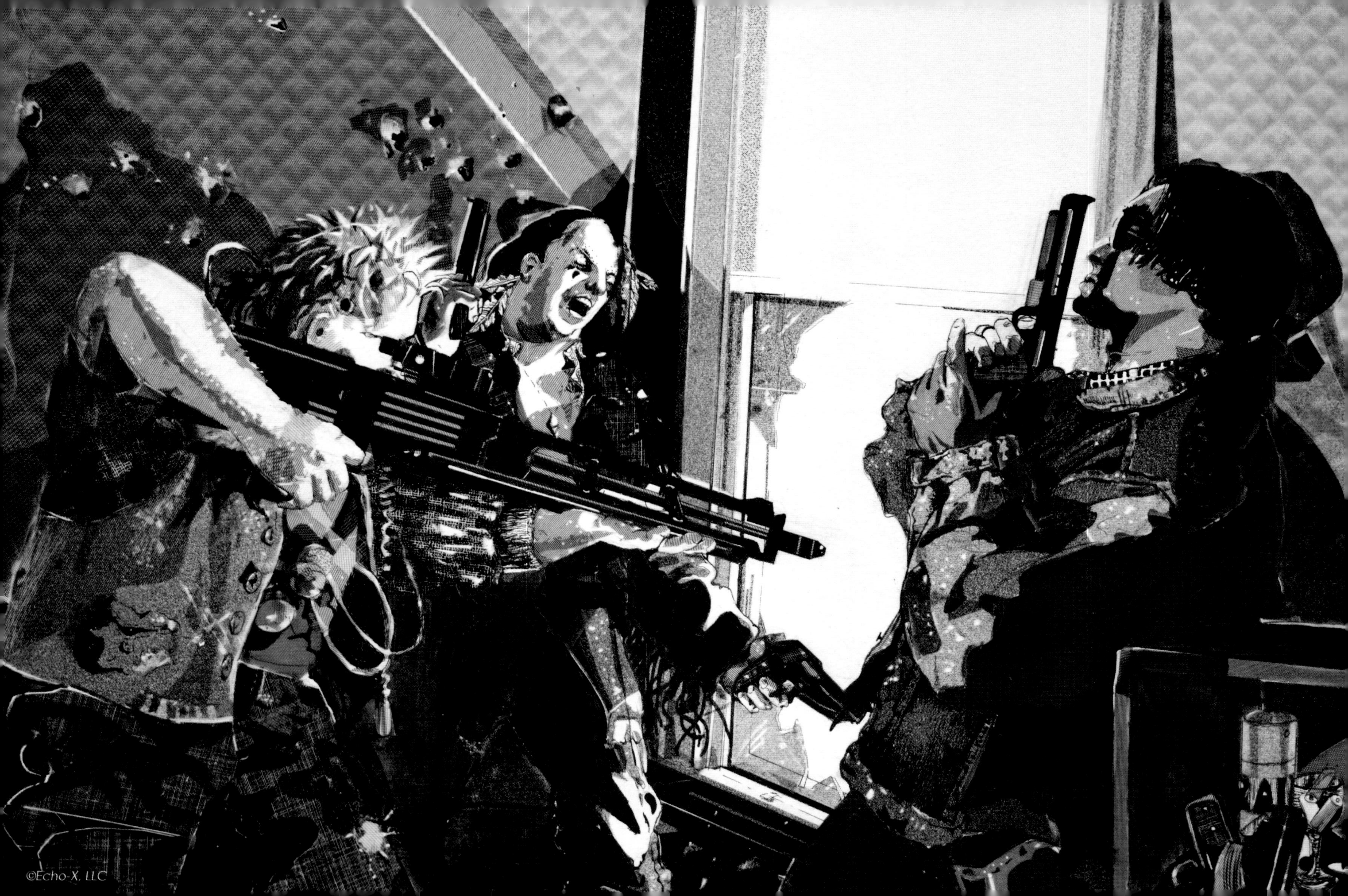

The Window

In my Junior year, I decided definitively that I wanted to illustrate right out of college. I was determined not to be sucked into a staff job and possibly lose my way - but instead, to jump full force into the freelance life. I've never been one for the cautious safe road.

We had a wide variety of role-playing books containing the work of Tim Bradstreet, Jeff Laubenstein, Mark Nelson, Janet Aulisio, and a host of others who were working magic in black and white. At school, no one worked in black and white, and yet most of the early publishing opportunities were for interiors. So, I focused my efforts on learning various monochromatic techniques with the intent to be published before leaving college.

I had heard of a product called Letratone by Letraset from some of my architectural friends. It is essentially a large sheet of transparent tape with various black patterns printed on it. I recruited Lazarus and the rest of my Shadowrun group to model for me. We didn't even have props at the time. I shot my own reference with black and white film, and developed it in our closet darkroom.*

By painstakingly cutting and placing hundreds of layers upon layers over a period of 30 hours, I achieved The Window. It was a huge boost to my portfolio - and with it I won recognition from my professors and landed my first paying illustration job for White Wolf, while still in school.

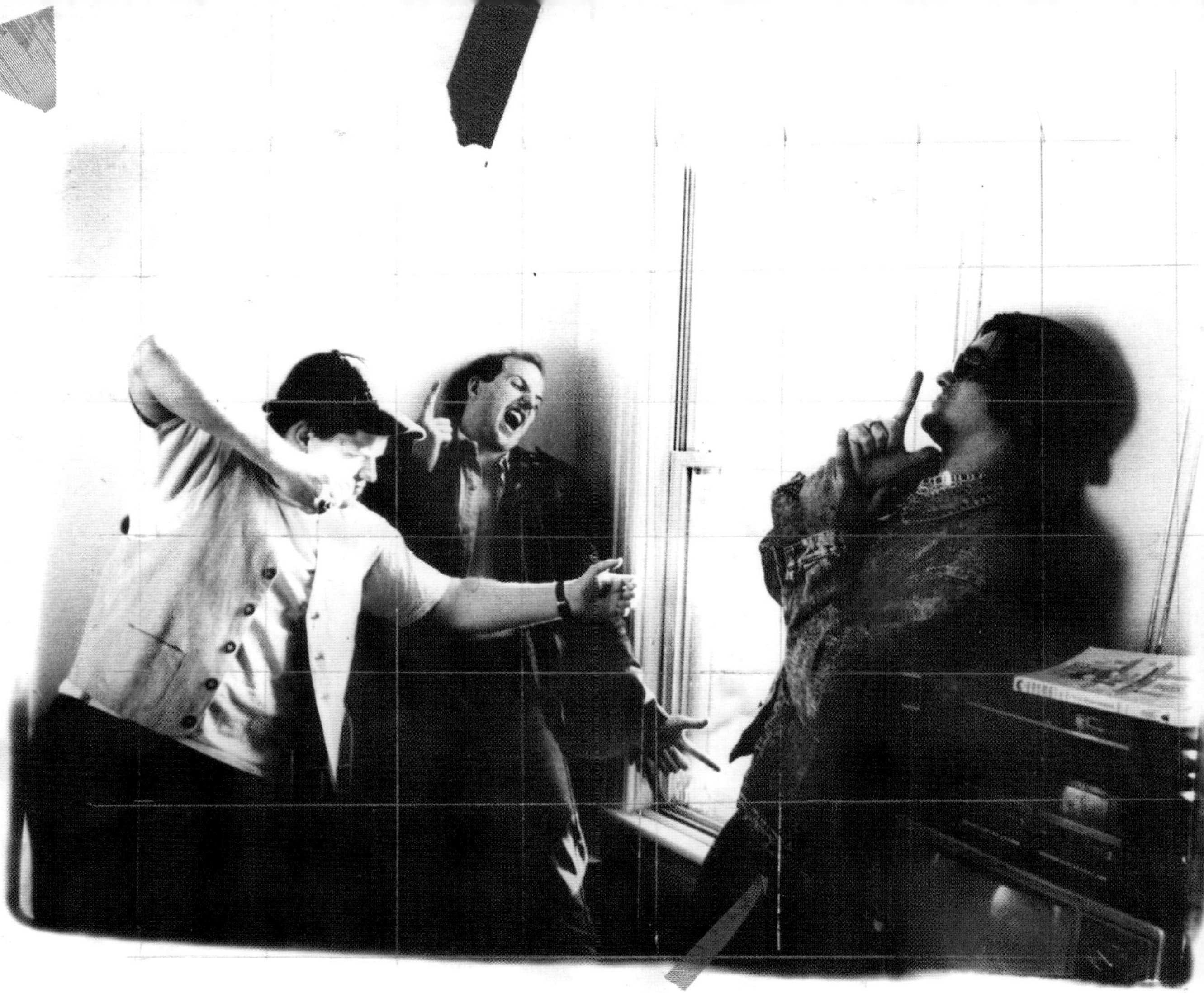

This was taken in the living room of Lazarus' first apartment in Brooklyn.

* *It confused more than one realtor that I used walk-in closet space as a darkroom.*

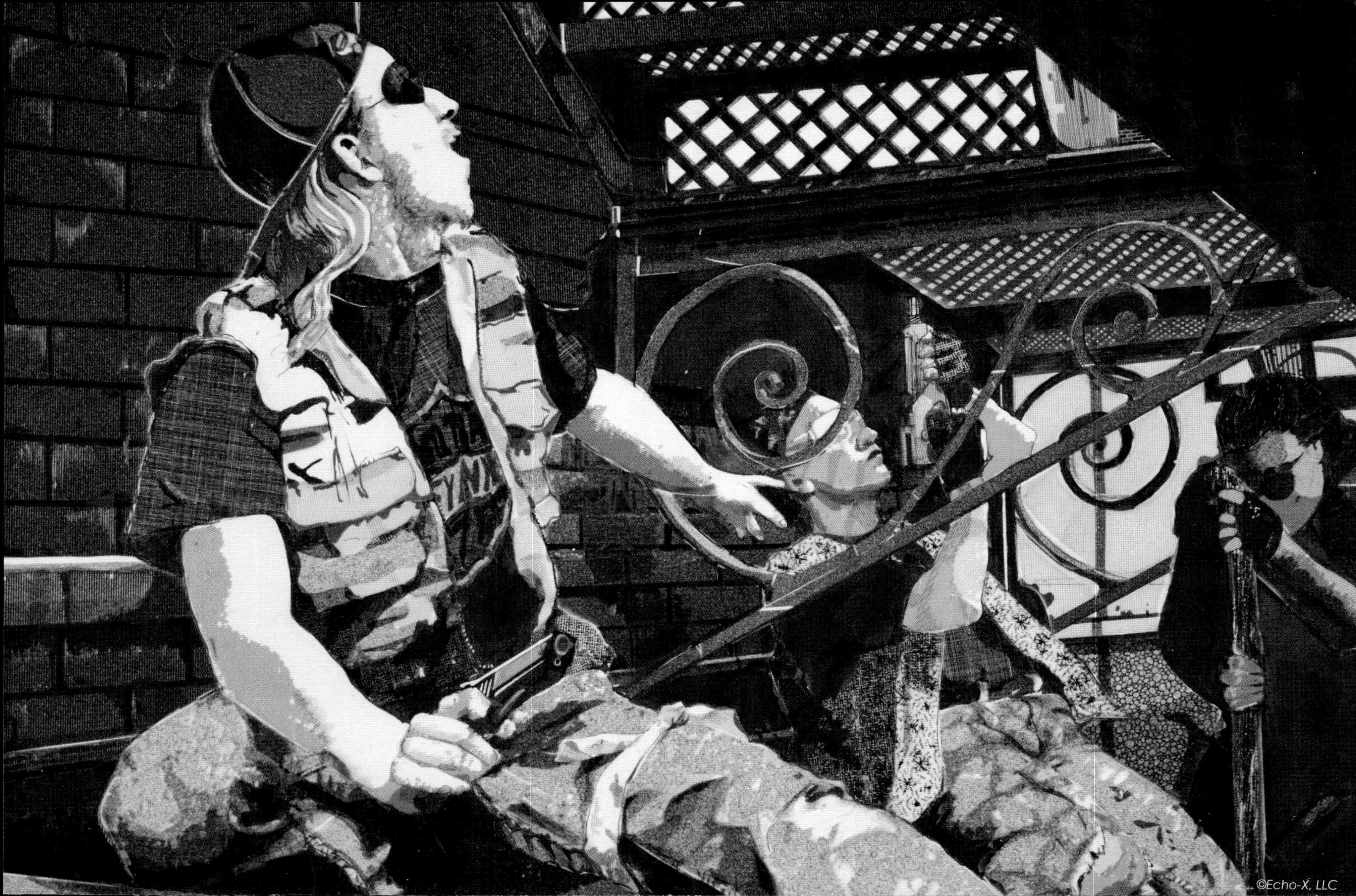

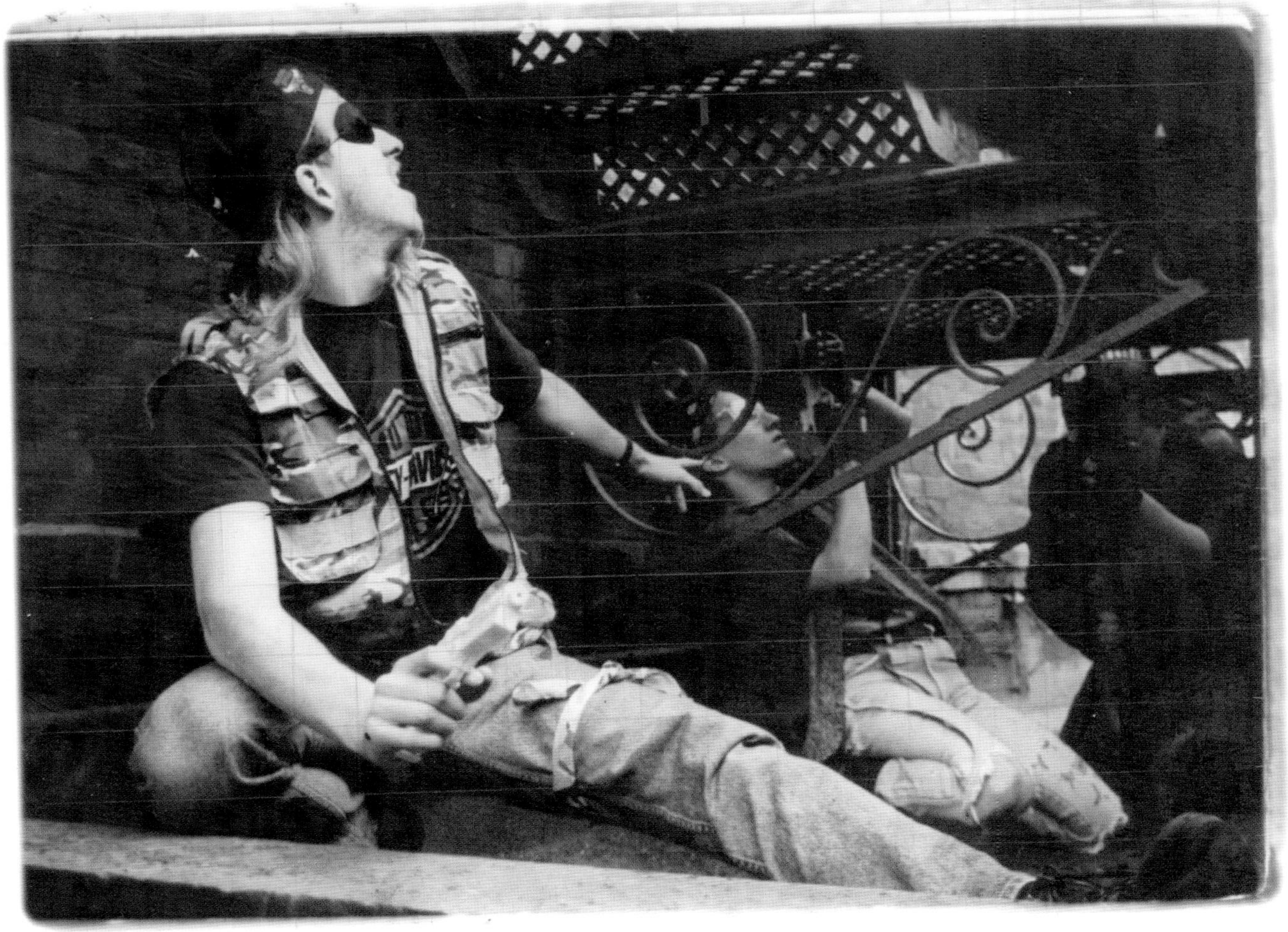

At one time, Lazarus had really long hair.

Stairs

This is the second in my series learning Letratone for my portfolio. The Window and Stairs are both considered my earliest pieces in my style, and were landmark for earning me published work.

It was less than week after The Window, and I was really getting a feel for what I could and couldn't do with the cut and stick medium. This time, I was much better at slicing it, flaking awcy, and playing with details and tones.

The photograph I took was also much better in tonality and composition to begin with. The art school we went to was designed to be a shoe factory at the end of the 19th century, so not only did it have all these amazingly industrial alleys and rooftops - the gates, scaffolds, and stairs were ornamental hand-worked iron.

Those of you familiar with my Art Nouveau works will see that even here - in such an early work, I was really attracted to exquisite details.

Among my models were Lazarus and his roommate Christian (far right).

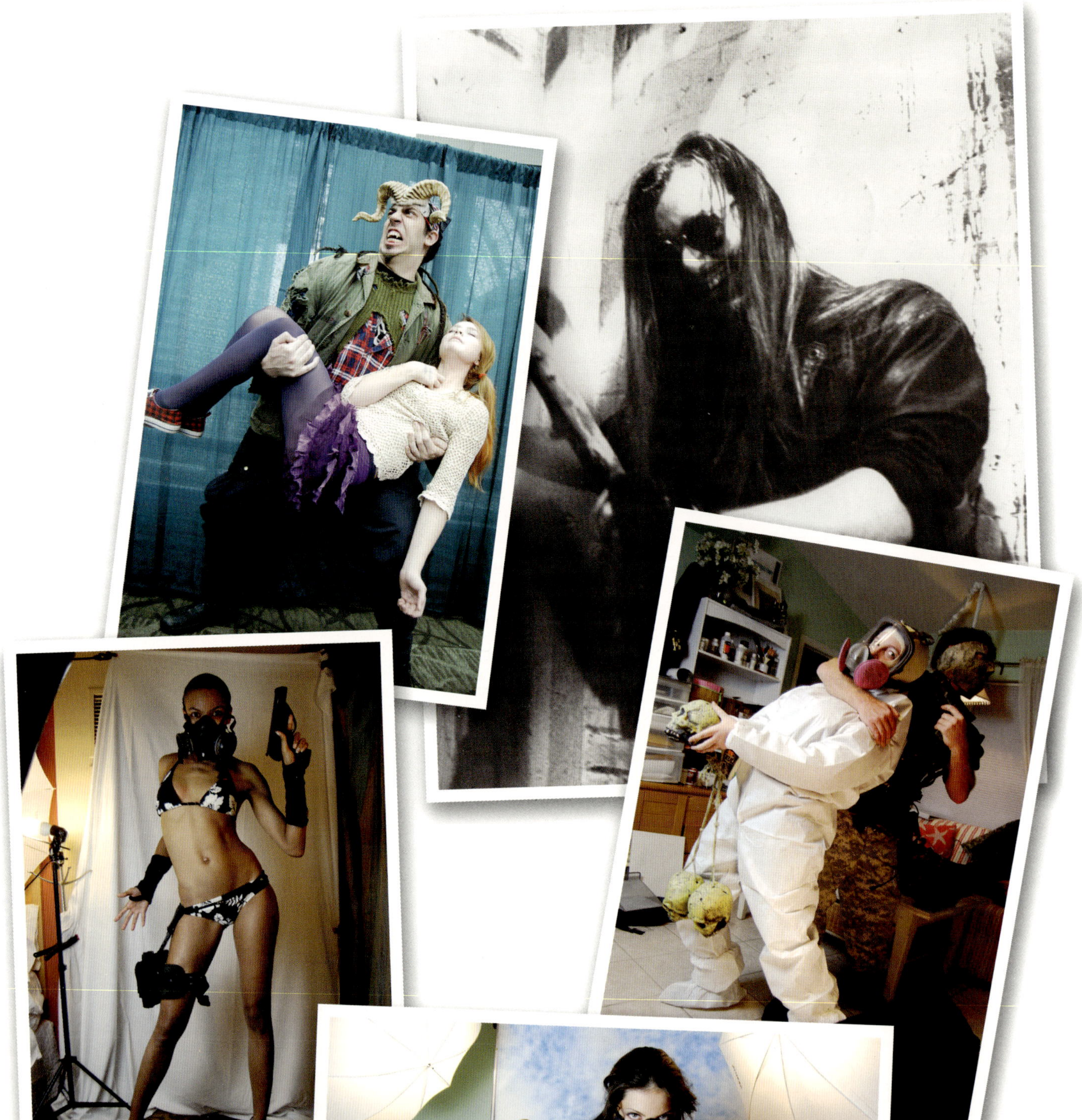

MODELS/ASSISTANTS

Sean "Raven" Ambrioso
Ryan "Mach" Bobnik
Marie-Claude Bourbonnais
Angela Chancey
Katheryn Chernik
Lazarus "The Deep" Chernik
Runa Chernik
Jesse "Bubbles" Cooper
"Dane Bramage"
Megan "Choose" Deputy
Christian "but not really" Fuller
Ember Johnston
Visceral "Storm" Krystal
Yaya Han
Harlequin*
Chris "Chuck Finley" Hawes
Roxana "Cupcake" Hire
Holly "Codename: My Mom" McKinney
Mandy "Nuts" Ng
Ashley "Ahro"Oliva
Meghan "The Muse" Perkins
Eric "Wotan" Pope
Denise "Valentine" Ritenour
Selena
Shambrea
Tara Ryze
Chad Seymour
Kathy "Gin" Shearer
Darla Varga
John "Schick" Viator
Alain Viesca
Zach "Fiero Suavé" Yurian
Zeppo
William "Just Some Guy" Zylstra

...and so more over the years.
Thank you, all.

*as himself

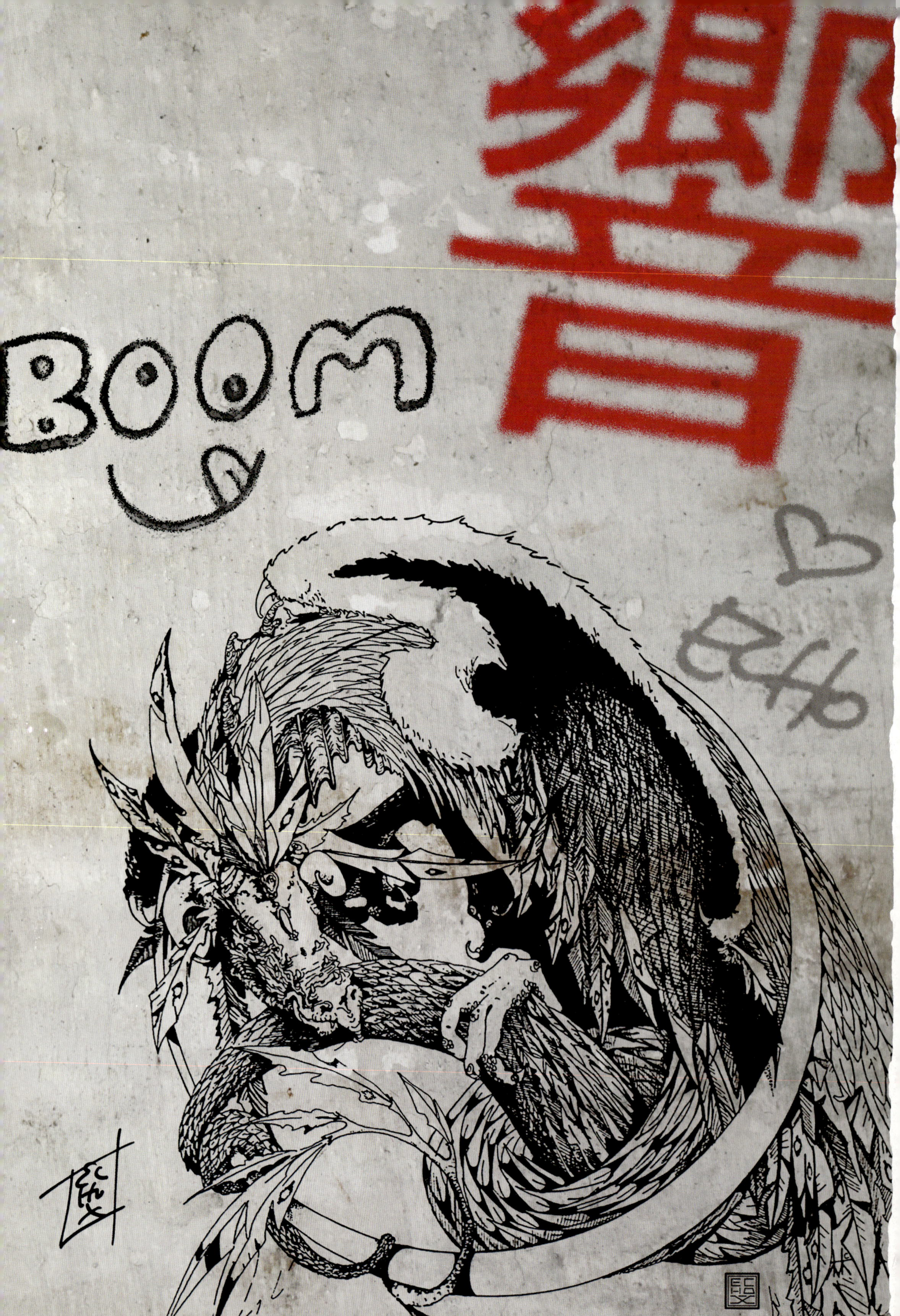
響
Boom
Echo